KATHY SUE MILLER WAS A BEAUTIFUL 16-YEAR-OLD INNOCENT WHEN SHE ANSWERED THE INVITING JOB AD.

WHEN THE POLICE FOUND HER, EVEN THEY WERE SHOCKED. . . .

What made the crime even more maddening for Seattle police detectives Billy Baughman and Duane Homan was that they knew who the killer was, yet could not arrest him. They were just the first of the frustrated police detectives who tried to stop Harvey Louis Carignan, a man whose power over his succession of wives and girlfriends sealed their lips, whose skill in removing physical evidence of guilt was near perfect, and whose courtroom brilliance used our laws to protect him from justice.

In all the annals of American crime, there has been no killer more terrifying in his abuse of women . . . and in his abuse of our legal system.

D0027738

ANN RULE is a former policewoman who has worked as a true-crime writer for many years, with articles in a host of magazines. In addition, she has lectured widely at law-enforcement schools and agencies. She is regarded as one of the nation's foremost experts on the subject of serial murders. Her bestselling books, *The Stranger Beside Me*, *Possession*, *Small Sacrifices*, and *Lust Killer* are available in Signet editions.

THE WANT-AD KILLER

ANN RULE
(WRITING AS ANDY STACK)

Updated Edition

A SIGNET BOOK

NEW AMERICAN LIBRARY

PUBLISHED BY
PENGUIN BOOKS CANADA LIMITED

NAL BOOKS ARE AVAILABLE AT QUANTITY DISCOUNTS
WHEN USED TO PROMOTE PRODUCTS OR SERVICES.
FOR INFORMATION PLEASE WRITE TO PREMIUM MARKETING DIVISION,
NEW AMERICAN LIBRARY, 1633 BROADWAY,
NEW YORK, NEW YORK 10019.

Copyright © 1983, 1988 by Ann Rule

First Printing, September, 1983
Fourth Printing, (*First Printing*, Revised Edition), November, 1988

5 6 7 8 9

SIGNET TRADEMARK REG. U.S. PAT OFF AND FOREIGN COUNTRIES
REGISTERED TRADEMARK — MARCA REGISTRADA
HECHO EN WINNIPEG, CANADA

SIGNET, SIGNET CLASSIC, MENTOR, ONYX, PLUME,
MERIDIAN and NAL BOOKS are published in Canada by Penguin
Books Canada Limited, 2801 John Street, Markham, Ontario,
Canada L3R 1B4
PRINTED IN CANADA
COVER PRINTED IN U.S.A.

This book is dedicated to the Families and Friends of Missing Persons and Violent Crime Victims, Seattle, Washington—with the author's deepest respect for those who have coped with disaster and changed it into hope.

And to Gwen Burton, who had the courage to testify in open court against Harvey Louis Carignan. Without Gwen's testimony, there might have been no convictions.

ACKNOWLEDGMENTS

This book could not have been written without the help of the following individuals and organizations. Although recalling events was both onerous and painful for many of those who helped me, it is my hope that the resulting work meets with their approval. My sincere thanks to: Mary Miller, Linda Barker, Doreen Hanson, Sally Peterson, and Lola Lindstad of the Families and Friends of Missing Persons and Violent Crime Victims; Detectives Duane Homan, Billy Baughman, Dick Reed, Wayne Dorman, and Don Cameron of the Seattle Police Department's Homicide Unit; Detective Archie Sonenstahl of the Hennepin County, Minnesota, Sheriff's Office; and to George Ishii, director of the Western Washington Crime Lab. Special thanks go to Pierce Brooks, retired captain of detectives of the Los Angeles Police Department, and Robert Heck of the U.S. Department of Justice, designers of VI-CAP, the Violent Criminal Apprehension Program.

My appreciation to my editor, Michael Ossias, and my agents, Joan and Joe Foley.

And to Mike Prezbindowski, president of Systems West, whose skill provided me, finally, with a word-processing system!

Prologue

Mary Miller had a terrible nightmare in the late summer of 1957, a dream so real that she woke in terror in the humid heat of that New York City August night, a dream so full of the portent of evil yet to come that it clung tenaciously to the cobwebby places of the mind where conscious thought rarely surfaces. She would never dream that dream again, and yet she never really forgot it; it walked with her, whispering of tragedy, for the next fifteen years.

And then, just when she thought that it was really only a nightmare after all, it came true.

Mary Miller was twenty-five when the nightmare came, a young wife, a new mother. Only twenty-five, and yet she had already lived through disaster and loss, and somehow survived. When she was still Mary Purgalis, she had lived the comfortable childhood given to upper-middle-class European children before the Second World War changed everything. Born in Latvia, in a little town almost on the Russian border, to parents who were both highly respected judges, and cosseted by a close and loving extended family, Mary Purgalis, the child, knew only happy memories. With the invasive onslaught of the German and Russian armies, that life was blown away like dandelion fluff in a sudden wind.

"When the war came, we had to leave Riga—the capital of Latvia—and try to find a way west. The Russians came in, and then the Germans, and then the Russians again, and nothing was the same. We had tried to get to Sweden but we couldn't make the border, so we just kept heading west, walking, and riding coal trains when we could. We were all together," Mary recalls. "I was a kid; I didn't really know how bad it was. My parents, my sisters and brother, my great-aunt, my grandmother—all of us—heading for Dresden. But when we got there, Dresden had been flattened. We were supposed to leave on a boat—but it sank. There was little food. People think that hunger hurts, but it doesn't. After a while, you don't even notice; you only get sick when you have something to eat again."

Mary Miller skips over her "war stories." "They don't matter. What happened to Kathy was so much worse than anything that happened to me in the war. We weren't in a concentration camp; we were in a displaced-persons camp. And then there was a sponsor who brought us all to America, to the state of Washington. We were all still together, and it was okay then."

Mary Purgalis started school at Clover Park High School in Tacoma, Washington, a stranger in a strange land where she barely understood the language. She had learned English in Latvia, but "American" English was different from what she had learned in textbooks.

"I had enough credits to graduate from high school, but I had to learn to speak the language, so I took English and American history, and all the subjects I'd never had before."

She learned rapidly; she was very bright, and even then had a strength, a resilience that belied her frail appearance.

"I went to school with the children of the guards from the federal prison at McNeil Island. I thought that was as close as I would ever come to crime or violence in America. We lived on Anderson Island, a tiny island that lies just off Tacoma in Puget Sound. The last ferry back to the island was at seven P.M. We knew several Latvian doctors who worked at the state mental hospital—Western Washington State Hospital—so if we wanted to participate in school functions in the evening or go to the movies, we slept over at the hospital. It didn't have the sexual offenders' program then, of course. They were just sick, sad, people.

"I wasn't afraid."

After Mary Purgalis graduated from high school, she moved to New York City—"Because that's where I thought everyone went to seek their fortunes." She married, and on May 23, 1957, she gave birth to her first child: a daughter, Katherine Sue Miller.

Kathy was born in the French Hospital in New York. She was a beautiful, healthy, blond baby.

The nightmare came when Kathy was four months old.

"I dreamed that I had a daughter with long dark hair. She was fourteen years old in my dream, and someone had hurt her. There was blood all over her face. I couldn't tell if she was dead, but I knew that she was terribly hurt. There was so much blood, and try as I might, I couldn't help her. . . ."

The residue of the nightmare stayed with Mary Miller all the while Kathy grew up. Even though the Millers moved around the country, the dream traveled with Mary. She was relieved to see that Kathy's hair stayed very blond—that she did not have a daughter with dark hair.

Still, she was always extra careful with Kathy. She checked on her safety frequently, more as the little girl grew into adolescence. When Kathy was old enough to baby-sit, Mary dropped in to be sure that everything was all right. She warned her about strangers, about hitchhiking, about tragedies that happened to other young girls.

"Maybe I warned her too much, but I was still afraid. After Kathy turned fifteen, I didn't worry so much. She had long blond hair, not dark hair like the daughter in my dream. And she wasn't fourteen anymore. I thought that we'd somehow gotten past whatever waited for us in that dream."

Still, Mary carefully read stories from the newspapers out loud to Kathy, articles about young women who had met with tragedy. In the fall of 1972, Mary and her children were living in Seattle, and Washington papers were full of coverage about the disappearance of a pretty young college student, Laura Leslie Brock.

Laura Brock had vanished while hitchhiking from Western Washington State University in Bellingham to Whidbey Island. When Laura Brock's nude body was found hidden in a dense fir forest on the island, Island County detectives had sought possible witnesses. They found a couple who had seen Laura Brock—or someone answering her description—hitching a ride beside the road, and then getting into a Chevrolet pickup truck with a male driver.

"I read all those articles to Kathy, and she told me she would never think of hitchhiking, and I know that she wouldn't have."

On the last weekend of April 1973, Kathy returned to her North Seattle home very frightened. A man had followed the slender teenager as she walked from the pool at the University of Washington, where she was taking swimming lessons.

Kathy was sure that he had been just behind her, turning corners when she did, and following her to the bus stop. She had been frightened enough to run all the way home.

"She was scared, and I was scared," Mary remembers. "I told her that I would go to the pool with her the next weekend, just in case he came back. Only, the next weekend never came. Kathy was dead by then. . . ."

I

Washington

I

Harvey Louis Carignan's birthday was in May—just as Kathy Miller's was, possibly the only thing they shared in common. Harvey Carignan was born on May 18, 1927. He did not celebrate that day in 1957, five days before Kathy's birth. He had little to celebrate; he was locked up in the federal penitentiary on Alcatraz Island off the coast of California. He had served only six years of a fifteen-year sentence, and his future hardly looked promising. But then again, he sometimes considered himself a lucky man. He'd made it to the age of thirty, and that hadn't seemed probable in 1950. The Territory of Alaska had sentenced him to hang, and only some skilled legal maneuvering had saved him. Compared to the gallows, even bleak Alcatraz, "The Rock," was a happier alternative.

Harvey was a big man, a hulking six-feet-two, weighing 190 pounds. His normal expression could only be described as glowering. He seldom smiled. No one bugged him in Alcatraz. He was very frightening when he was angry, and he was not known for his even temper. The other cons gave him a wide berth. He considered that he had no friends—only acquaintances. He was not close to his family.

Harvey Carignan was born in Fargo, North Dakota—just across the Red River from the Minnesota state line. His birth was illegitimate, an occurrence that, in 1927, carried with it far more stigma than it does today. Family lore reveals that Harvey's father was a medical intern, a man of some brilliance,

15

but nothing more. "It would hurt too many people to talk about it now" is all a relative will say about Harvey's father.

Although Harvey would never learn who his genetic father was, he would come to consider that his stepfather was his father, a somewhat tenuous relationship, but the only father-son relationship available. Whoever his natural father was, he would be gone from Harvey's world long before the toddler could comprehend what was going on. His adult recall would reach back to the time he was just under four, and no further.

The first home Harvey remembers was near Backoo, North Dakota. That would have been in 1930, when the Great Depression was at its lowest ebb. His mother, barely twenty, was ill-equipped to support herself, much less her nervous, skinny little son. Jobs in Backoo, North Dakota, were not plentiful in 1930, not even for a man with a trade. Harvey remembers very little from those early years. He remembers that his grandmother bought him shoes, and he remembers a hired girl, or perhaps only a girl who lived with the family. Few of his early memories are pleasant.

Harvey was undersized, a child who failed to thrive, and something of a behavior problem. His small features would twitch unbidden when he was under stress, and he wet the bed long after he should have been trained. He felt unloved, and unlovable.

There are huge gaps in his memory of his first eleven years, but there is a continuing thread of early terror that lies entrenched in his consciousness. He is adamant when he says that, early on, he was the object of sexual abuse from women. Grown women. It may be that his recall is flawed by his bizarre adult aberrations. It may be that he remembers correctly. It is only in the last few years that child abuse has been exposed as the epidemic social blight that it is. Not only female children are victims. If Harvey is telling the truth, he was the victim of a great deal of inappropriate sexual behavior before he reached puberty. Female breasts and genitals became weapons used to smother and suffocate him rather than objects of comfort and erotic fulfillment.

Harvey's mother married when he was about four, and he

remembers that she gave birth to a second child, another son. This son had a father who was his own; Harvey did not.

Asked about his mother in a court hearing many, many years later, he said, "She was pretty mean."

Again, only his perception? Or perhaps accurate memory?

He will not admit to hating his mother, and explains that "I don't like a lot of things she did—but I don't hate her, no. . . ."

To his attorneys, when he was well over forty, Harvey allegedly confided instances of sexual abuse perpetrated by a female relative, but in court he demurred when asked to describe the instances, insisting that those revelations had been made in strictest privacy.

He would testify, however, that a baby-sitter "rubbed herself all over me," and that it bothered him. He had not understood what she was doing to him, but he had sensed that it was not right. He only learned, apparently, that women could hurt him and make him full of anxiety. The spindly child repressed his rage and revulsion. There was nothing else he could do. Not at that time, anyway. . . .

His bed-wetting became chronic. This was not acceptable in his home, and he was sent away to live with an aunt and uncle in Cavalier, North Dakota, another hamlet, hard by the Canadian border. He recalls that he thought he was fitting into that household well. He was surprised when his aunt and uncle told him he could not stay, that he had to go home to his mother and stepfather.

Not yet eleven, he lasted only a few months in his mother's home, and then he was shipped off again. He went to live with his grandmother in Williams, Minnesota. The older woman was dismayed by his bed-wetting too, and decided she could not cope with it.

He went next to live with another of his maternal aunts, who also lived in Williams. Homesick, Harvey ran away after a short time—back to his mother.

Besides suffering enuresis, Harvey was, early on, a thief. He stole a bicycle and other, smaller items. In his own recall of his problems, he consistently fails to mention these thefts, and seems adept at blocking them.

He does describe attitudes that he developed to support a fragile ego. He notes that he was a prodigious reader, and "always mentally ahead of my companions." He was shy and silent. "I'd have to steel myself to talk, and when I would talk—especially in anger, which was often—I'd be vituperative and mean. If I couldn't have friends, I'd have a reputation that they couldn't ignore even if they didn't admire it. They'd notice me one way or the other. All my life that has been my way; when someone did not give me attention I thought I deserved, I'd reach out and slap them—either with words or with my hands. That was my way of making sure they didn't ignore me, treat me as if I didn't exist. If they didn't or couldn't love me, I made sure they hated me. I had to be foremost in their minds."

Not surprisingly, this attitude did little to endear Harvey to his family or peers. He was a prickly pear of a child, bounced from one household to another.

His own preference—indeed, his obsession—was to be home with his mother, but he was unwelcome there. He may have been a living reminder of her abandonment by the young doctor who fathered him. It may only have been that she could not deal with this intelligent but perverse child.

"I was home about two months and my mother tried to put me in an orphanage, only there wasn't any—so they put me in the reform school. Over in Mandan, North Dakota. I stayed there seven years."

Harvey Carignan'S FBI "rap sheet" notes this as the first entry: "North Dakota Training School: Delinquent. 1939 to 1946."

Harvey states that it was his mother who had finally thrown up her hands and decided that she could not keep him in the family home. His stepfather had tried to talk her out of it, to give Harvey one more chance.

"My mother told the judge that she couldn't keep me, and my stepdad said, 'Well, we can try,' and she said, 'No, we can't keep him,' and the judge, he says, 'Well, being he needs this treatment and you can't pay for it, I think we will send him to Mandan.' "

Harvey's ailment, the problem that he says caused him to

be locked up in a boys' reform school for seven years, was Saint Vitus's dance—or childhood chorea—a disease which manifests itself with spasmodic jerking movements the sufferer cannot control. It may have been psychogenic in nature; the pathology of the disease is difficult to isolate.

The specter of mental illness haunted Harvey's mother. There had been instances of psychosis in the family background. She may have seen her son's constant twitching movements as a sign that he was, indeed, "crazy."

She signed the papers and Harvey went off to Mandan.

The scrawny eleven-year-old found reform school a frightening place.

"I guess overall I got along pretty good there. When I first got there, I had some problems—guys beating up on me. I was pretty small. And so they took another guy and me—he was also very small—and they kind of gave us a separate room. That took care of the problem in a way, except that the guys used to tease me and stuff like that."

Discipline inside the walls at Mandan was, according to Harvey, meted out by the female members of the staff.

"There were both men and women running the place, but mostly women. A lot of times, they'd punish you for no reason. And the way they would do it would be funny. They would hold you up against their breasts or their stomachs, or something, like they were trying to choke you and stuff like that."

In trying to make some sense out of Harvey's later crimes, it is perhaps more relevant to view his perception of the way women treated him when he was a child and a teenager rather than to attempt to verify that his version of the facts is correct. He grew to adulthood firmly convinced that women controlled his life, and that those women he encountered were often seductive, sexually abusive giantesses who could use him for their own purposes whenever they wished. It is possible that none of it ever happened—not the female relative who played with him sexually, nor the baby-sitter, nor the women in the training school in Mandan. True or not, he believed that all these things occurred, and that he was powerless to stop the incidents. At the same time, such abuse would have been sexually stimulating, propelling him too young into a sexual life long before he was mature enough to cope with the feelings that ensued.

Raised a Roman Catholic, Harvey had also been indoctrinated with the taboos of the church, the concept of original sin, and the edict that women are to be revered and respected.

He could not understand why such evil things had been done to him by women.

Harvey stayed in Mandan throughout most of his puberty; the Second World War had passed by somewhere out in the world he was no part of. In 1946, that war was history, and Harvey's seven-year "sentence" was over. He was eighteen, and it was time to send him out into the community. He had not lived a normal life . . . nor would he ever. He no longer wet his bed. He still twitched when the tension was too great.

Institutionalized for so many years, Harvey immediately signed up to join another institution: the United States Army.

The Army welcomed him. He was no longer a rabbit-faced child; he had grown tall through all those years at Mandan, fattened on the high-carbohydrate diet dear to dietitians who must feed large groups of people. Still, he'd had enough protein from the training-school farm that he was not ill-nourished.

Ill-prepared, possibly, but not ill-nourished.

In 1948, both Harvey Carignan and Mary Purgalis had reason to pass through Seattle. Mary, rescued from the wasteland that much of Europe had become, journeyed through Seattle on her way to Anderson Island, where she would start her new life. And Harvey traveled through the Queen City of the Northwest on his way to his new Army assignment at Fort Richardson in Anchorage, Alaska.

They did not, of course, meet. They were not to meet for another twenty-five years.

Sunday, July 31, 1949, was a day full of light in Anchorage, Alaska—only something over one month removed from the summer solstice in the land of the midnight sun. When John Keith walked toward his home in Anchorage shortly after nine P.M. that Sunday, the sky was still blue and the shadows had scarcely lengthened.

Keith, intent on his own thoughts, suddenly became aware of some sound coming from a small park off to his right. He turned and looked toward the direction of the noise. A cry for help? A grunting, strange sound, it had been, something he could not readily identify. He saw a couple in the park, a man and a woman lying on the grass. Thinking that the woman might have cried out for assistance, Keith stepped from the roadside and headed toward the couple.

As Keith approached, the man rose up from the grassy slope and angrily told him to "Move on!"

Embarrassed, Keith assumed that he had encountered the couple in the act of intercourse, although the park seemed to him to be a little public for making love in the bright evening light. He backed off, and continued on toward his home. He had seen the man quite clearly. A big man, with slightly receding brown hair, although he had appeared to be only in his early twenties. Keith could not say why he felt so uneasy. People did occasionally make love in public, especially when they were young and they had had a few drinks. The woman had not called out again as he approached the pair, had seemingly gone along with the man. Perhaps she had been embarrassed to be discovered in such dishabille. Keith finally fell asleep, almost convinced that *he* had been the intruder, thoughtlessly poking his nose into a private interlude.

Keith walked by the park at six the next morning as he headed for the downtown section of Anchorage. Something made him walk over to the little park where he had seen the amorous couple. The man was gone, but the woman lay there still. He could see now why she had not moved or said anything to him nine hours before.

She was dead.

Keith could hardly bear to look at her. She was no longer young, although Keith was sure that the man had been. This dead woman had to be over forty, perhaps even older. She was partially nude, and it looked as if her clothing had been forcibly ripped off. Her face was purplish black and swollen grotesquely.

Keith wasted no time in notifying the Anchorage police, and soon crews of investigators were at the park, staring down at the beaten body of the dead woman.

The victim was in a state of full rigor mortis, all of her limbs stiffened and cold. The pathologist who performed the autopsy on the woman estimated that she had died sometime the evening before. Death had occurred because of severe brain damage from a tremendous bludgeoning. Her face had been virtually destroyed from the chin to the forehead, bone and tissue crushed to a pulp. The weapon—or weapons—had unquestionably been human fists. Bruising on the victim's inner thighs and genitalia indicated that the dead woman had probably been killed during a rape attempt, although penetration had not been accomplished. There was no semen present in the vaginal vault, and none appeared on her clothing when it was tested with acid phosphatase. Thus there was no way to determine the blood type of her attacker.

The woman in the park was subsequently identified as Laura Showalter, fifty-seven. Mrs. Showalter had not returned to her home on the night of July 31, and relatives and friends identified the battered corpse.

John Keith offered as much information as he could to the Anchorage detectives and to U.S. Marshal Herring. But there wasn't much. He described the young man he had seen lying in the grass with the victim, but he was positive he had never seen the man before. No, he was certain that he would have recognized the man if he had known him; he had walked close to the couple before the man bellowed at him to move on. The man had been very angry, an emotion that Keith had thought normal enough—considering the circumstances as he had perceived them at the time. He had not come any closer, but walked on with his head averted.

Laura Showalter was buried, and the case was at a standstill for several weeks. There were so many men moving through Anchorage, some seeking their fortunes in Alaska, some stationed at Fort Richardson.

On Friday September 16 a young woman named Dorcas Callen was confronted by a soldier on an Anchorage street. She stood on the street near a tavern, and the soldier seemed intoxicated, although it was only eleven o'clock in the morning. When the man asked Dorcas to take a ride with him, she refused and turned away.

"Hey," the man continued. "I think I know you . . . maybe."

"Please go away," Dorcas pleaded. "You *don't* know me."

She was frightened now. She knew that a woman had been beaten to death in the neighborhood only weeks before. But the husky soldier was angered by her refusal, and she could not get away from him. Before she could move, the man grabbed her and began to drag her away from the street. They fell into a ditch beside the road, and he was all over her, tearing at her clothing, his hands touching her on her breasts, between her legs. In another minute, he would rape her.

Dorcas fought him, fighting frantically to find a handhold in the soft dirt walls of the ditch. He was very strong, almost inhumanly strong. Screaming, she managed to clamber out of the pit. She ran across the street toward the tavern.

Dorcas Callen was more fortunate than Laura Showalter had been; she managed to get away from the would-be rapist, bruised and bleeding—but alive. She immediately reported the assault to the Anchorage police. She was able to give them an accurate description, right down to the deep dimple in the rapist's chin. Police searched the area, and later on that Friday afternoon, they found a young soldier who resembled Dorcas' attacker even to the dimple in his chin. They brought Harvey Louis Carignan, twenty-two, into the station.

Carignan, who gave his address as the barracks at Fort Richardson, was placed in a lineup with four other men of similar size and coloring. Dorcas Callen viewed the lineup and searched the faces of the men standing there.

She picked Harvey Carignan at once.

Dorcas' statement on the attempted rape sounded familiar to the detectives working on the Showalter murder. Someone had killed Laura Showalter in an abortive sexual assault, and she too had been beaten with bare fists. The M.O. was almost identical to the Callen assault. Both women had been approached by their attacker on a weekend day, and both men had been big, young, and brown-haired. It sounded close enough to arrange for John Keith to come in and view the lineup.

Keith looked the five men over and then picked Harvey Carignan as the man who "looked nearer like the man I saw there [next to Laura Showalter's body] than any man I have seen."

And so Harvey Carignan, three years out of the Mandan reformatory, was placed under arrest on the charge of assault to commit rape on Dorcas Callen. He was booked into the Anchorage city jail.

Carignan admitted the attempted rape, but he did not want to talk about the Showalter case.

Although the Miranda decision regarding the reading of rights to a suspect—his right to counsel, his right to remain silent, and his right to end an interrogation whenever he chooses—did not come into law until 1958, there were guidelines established for the prisoner's right to speedy arraignment and for interrogation procedure in 1949.

Harvey Carignan was just beginning his jousting with the justice system in America. As the years passed, he would become more and more adept at sidestepping the law.

On Saturday morning, September 17, 1949, the Anchorage police were frustrated with Harvey in their efforts to discuss the death of Laura Showalter. They took him to the office of U.S. Marshal Herring. Herring's reputation as a skilled interrogator was well established. If anyone could extract the truth about Laura Showalter's murder from Harvey, the consensus was that it would be Herring.

But the law is such a delicately balanced entity, and so many criteria must be met for judgments to survive the processes of appeal.

Already, a vital step had been omitted. Carignan had been swiftly brought before a magistrate and given a hearing on the Callen rape charge, and he had been advised of his rights in that case. A second hearing, however, had not been held regarding the murder charge. Indeed, he had not been charged in the death of Laura Showalter when he was taken to Herring's office.

Herring asked Harvey if he knew anything about the older woman's murder, or of how it could have happened. The young soldier would not talk about that crime, and asked to see a Catholic priest. He did not ask for an attorney, nor had Herring suggested that he might obtain counsel.

Marshal Herring located a priest, who did come to his office and who spoke in privacy with Harvey. When the priest left after an hour, Harvey said he wished to speak with Herring again.

Herring was a religious man, and he had long had several religious pictures on his office wall—prints of saints and of Jesus Christ. They had been there for years, so long that Herring never really thought about them. At the moment, he was intensely interested in finding out what his prisoner had to say, and the dusty pictures were invisible to him, part of the woodwork in his familiar office.

Herring looked at the prisoner and asked, "Are you ready to make a statement now, Harvey?"

"Yes."

"Well . . . ?"

"I want to do it in privacy. I need paper and pencil."

Herring gave Harvey a pad of paper and a fistful of pencils and he was taken back to his cell in the Anchorage jail and left alone. For all of that Saturday and Sunday, Harvey was undisturbed except for interruptions for meals. Herring called him once or twice to see how he was doing, and he replied that he was doing fine.

Harvey was treated well, as well as any prisoner. He was not beaten and he was not threatened or coerced into making a statement, only left alone with the tools he needed to transfer what was in his mind and on his conscience onto paper.

Herring felt some sympathy for the tall, gawky prisoner. He too had been raised in an orphanage—although he had chosen the law rather than crime when he was on his own. He tried to understand Harvey, but his mind always returned with a jolt to the scene of the Showalter murder. The woman had been beaten so savagely; it was hard to comprehend how anyone could have beaten a woman almost sixty, a frail woman at that . . . and beaten her until she was dead.

On Monday morning Harvey was brought again to Herring's office.

"Have you prepared a statement for me, Harvey?"

"Yes—but I need to see the priest again before I give it to you."

Again the priest was summoned, and again he remained closeted with Harvey for more than an hour.

When he left the office, the monsignor nodded at Herring. "He's ready now."

Harvey handed over a long statement, and Herring scanned it quickly and then read it carefully. There was nothing. Harvey had gone into great detail about the day and early evening of July 31. Most of his narrative concerned how much alcohol he had consumed that day bar-hopping with companions. Harvey hadn't mentioned the woman at all, and he certainly hadn't written anything about a murder. Nothing of attempted rape.

Nothing.

Herring looked up at the prisoner. "This isn't complete, Harvey. I asked you to tell me about how Laura Showalter died. You've only written about how drunk you got that day."

"I was afraid to say more because you might not believe me. I'm afraid my neck would stretch."

The death penalty—hanging on the gallows—was extant in the Territory of Alaska in 1949 and Harvey apparently knew it.

"We have had no hangings in the Anchorage judicial division since 1922," Herring told Harvey truthfully. "Not for twenty-seven years."

Herring told Harvey that he himself was not in a position to promise that there would be no hanging in this case, but the precedent *not* to hang had been set for almost three decades.

Seemingly relieved at that news, Harvey began to explore other possibilities. He was curious about the facilities at McNeil Island, the closest federal penitentiary. He wondered if he might have the opportunity to learn a trade if he should be confined there. Herring told him that he probably could.

Harvey seemed to like the marshal; he would not talk at all when other investigators were in the room. The two were communicating, although Harvey was still dragging his feet about giving specific details. Herring established some rapport when he talked of his own unhappy experiences as an orphan, confined in an institution. They did share that background, and Herring was able to empathize with Harvey's experiences. And yet he wanted mightily to avenge Laura Showalter. And to do that, he needed a confession.

By the end, they would have spent more than thirty hours together, exploring the parameters of the crime of murder.

The pictures of Christ and the saints gazed down on the two men as they talked. The marshal saw that Harvey glanced at them from time to time. And Herring went too far, although he would not realize it until later. He asked Harvey to look into the eyes of Christ.

"You can only set yourself right in the eyes of your Maker, Harvey, by confessing the true facts."

Harvey stared at the picture of Christ, saw the gentle eyes looking back at him, and he sighed. "All right, I'll tell you."

Yes, he had been drinking that day in July. He had encountered Laura Showalter, and she'd looked good to him. The alcohol had made her seem younger. No, he hadn't even thought about whether she was young or old. He hadn't even known her name. He'd wanted her. He had taken her to the park and attempted to have intercourse with her. When she'd balked, he'd beaten her with his fists until she didn't move.

Herring scribbled down the facts that Harvey dictated. It was all there now, the specifics of the brutal murder of a helpless victim.

When Harvey had signed the confession, Herring looked at him and said, "Harvey, you can still destroy this if you wish. It hasn't been out of this room."

Carignan shook his head. It was done, and he would leave the confession as it stood.

Harvey Carignan went on trial in the first months of 1950 for first-degree murder in the District Court for the Territory of

Alaska, Third Division, Justice George W. Folta presiding. The prosecution played their ace: the confession of murder given to Marshal Herring.

Harvey Carignan was convicted and sentenced to die on the gallows.

He was stunned; he had expected a sentence, instead, in NcNeil Island—where he could develop skills that would help him get a job when he was paroled. He certainly hadn't expected that he would hang when he'd confessed to Herring.

Harvey had spent four months in jail in Anchorage, and the Army had discharged him during that period. He was then moved to Seward, Alaska, where he would remain for ten months.

On December 8, 1950, Harvey's case came up on appeal before the Ninth Circuit of the United States Court of Appeals. Three judges—Justices Healy, Bone, and Pope—would listen to Attorney Harold J. Butcher of Anchorage, who was representing Harvey, and to U.S. Attorney J. Earl Cooper, who represented the Territory of Alaska. A majority decision—two out of the three justices—was needed to decide whether Harvey would hang or go free of the charges stemming from the murder of Laura Showalter.

Butcher argued that the confession made to Marshal Herring should not have been admitted into the lower court. Without the confession, there would have been no way to tie Harvey absolutely to the murder. He insisted that Herring had overstepped his bounds, and said the marshal had set himself up as a father confessor to an innocent, trusting young man. Further, he said that Harvey had been questioned without even being taken before the magistrate on the murder charge.

After days of testimony, two of the justices—Healy and Bone—ruled that the confession had been admitted in error. It was the only judgment they felt they could have made when the law was applied.

Justice Bone regretted that he had to rule for the defense, and made a statement that would jar detectives many years hence.

"We would be utterly naive if we overlooked the cold hard fact that we are not dealing with a simple, childlike mentality.

We deal with a cold-blooded rapist, who was clever and cunning enough to hide his criminal trail with great skill. He did not require the services of an attorney to know that he did not have to 'talk'—the record shows that he was advised of the Callen inquiry and fully understood that he could remain silent from the moment of his apprehension and detention on a criminal charge to the very end of the legal trial. His age and the extent of his literacy justifies the most careful appraisal of his understanding of the issues confronting him in the later Showalter matter. It will not do to rake and scrape through the whole gamut of possibilities to find some plausible reason to believe that he was a dull clod rather than a pretty smart criminal.''

Blocked by the dispassionate reality of the law, the Territory of Alaska took the case to the highest court in America in October 1951. The Supreme Court of the United States undertook the matter of Harvey Carignan's death sentence and its reversal by the Court of Appeals. Justices Reed, Douglas, Black, and Frankfurter agreed that Harvey Carignan's conviction had come about because the McNabb Rule (that confessions shall be excluded if obtained during an illegal detention due to failure to promptly carry a prisoner before a committing magistrate) had been violated.

And so it was done. The murder conviction had been appealed all the way to the Supreme Court and Harvey Carignan no longer faced the hangman's noose.

To try him again on the murder charge would put him in double jeopardy; beyond that, without his confession, they couldn't have hoped to convict him of murder anyway.

He was subsequently convicted of the attempted rape and assault on Dorcas Callen and drew a fifteen-year sentence. He was transferred from the Seward jail to McNeil Island, Washington.

For the four months he remained at McNeil Island, Harvey lived just across a narrow stretch of Puget Sound from Mary Purgalis; he was only one of thousands of prisoners locked up there. Mary never knew of his existence.

After four months, he was transferred again—this time to Alcatraz. Harvey earned some ''good time,'' and he served only nine years of his fifteen-year sentence. On April 2, 1960, he was paroled.

He was thirty-two years old. Except for his three years in the Army, Harvey had not walked free since he was eleven years old.

2

During the almost eleven years that Harvey Carignan was locked away in jails or prisons for the Dorcas Callen assault and near-rape, Mary Miller had moved several times. First to New York—where Kathy Sue was born. After Kathy's birth, the Millers settled in Salt Lake City, Utah. It was in Salt Lake, some seventeen months after Kathy's birth, that Mary had her second child: a son, Kenny.

Kathy had been quick to sit up, crawl, walk, and talk, but Kenny seemed slow to develop. He was a big, husky boy and Mary told herself that each child might be expected to mature at his own rate, that Kenny was slower because he was a boy. It did not occur to her then, although it would later, that Kenny had been born during the fallout from the atomic-energy tests on the Utah desert. It did not occur to anyone living in the area that there might be danger hiding in the great mushroom clouds that ballooned over the desert and then dissipated and fell to earth. It would be years before residents in the little Utah towns nearby began to succumb to cancer in proportions far greater than the average. Young wives miscarried, and babies were born with anomalies that could not be explained. Indeed, there would be speculation that the deaths of John Wayne, Susan Hayward, and Dick Powell, along with other members of the cast and crew of *The Conqueror*—a film about Genghis Khan that was shot on the Utah desert in 1956—might be traced to that lethal fallout.

"I don't know what happened when Kenny was born. I never will," Mary Miller says slowly. "It might have been

31

because of the fallout, or it might have been because my doctor left me alone and went out to dinner. I'm a fatalist, I guess. There seems to be a reason why things happen, and maybe we'll never know why it was meant to be. Kenny seemed fine, but as he grew older, we could see that his development was slow."

Kenny Miller would never catch up. When he was ready for kindergarten, Mary and her children lived in Seattle. "I took him to Children's Orthopedic Hospital for tests and they said he might try to go to regular kindergarten. It scared him half to death. He just sat there, so I put him in special education classes."

By this time the Millers' marriage had ended, and Mary had bought an older home in the north end of Seattle. Her grandmother Purgalis and great-aunt lived with them and looked after the children while Mary worked at a bank.

Mary Miller's parents lived only a few blocks away, and the children were more than welcome there too.

Kathy and Kenny were very close, and the little girl was protective of her younger brother, careful that no one should ever make fun of him or take advantage of him. Although things were not perfect in the home on 35th N.E., although there had been some bitter disappointments in Mary Miller's life, she still considered herself a lucky woman. Her extended family was still together.

And yet, for no reason she could rationally explain, Mary sometimes thought of the dream, and wondered if something terrible waited ahead, something she had no power to stop.

When Harvey Carignan walked away from Alcatraz, he had a new nickname, "Yankee," and a cheap suit furnished by the government. Harvey returned to Duluth, Minnesota, where one of his three half-brothers lived.

His time on the streets was short-lived. His FBI rap sheet shows that he was arrested on August 5, 1960, by officers of the Duluth Police Department. He had been free four months and three days.

The charges listed on the rap sheet are succinct: burglary and assault with intent to commit rape. He was convicted on only the burglary charge; the rape charge was apparently dropped for lack of evidence. As a parole violator, he was sentenced to 2,086 days in the federal prison at Leavenworth, Kansas, and given an additional suspended two-and-a-half-year sentence in the Minnesota State Penitentiary in Stillwater.

Harvey had yet to have any sort of long-term relationship with a woman. He had been shut away from women for most of his life. He denies any homosexual activity in prison, although he recalls that the "opportunity was always there."

When he was paroled from Leavenworth in 1964, Harvey left Minnesota behind and moved to Seattle, Washington. He had visited Seattle before. His mother and stepfather lived there now, as well as another of his half-brothers. He registered as a paroled convict in Seattle on March 2, 1964.

Geographically, he was now very close to Kathy Sue Miller, but Kathy was only six years old, a winsomely pretty, slender blond child.

Harvey didn't last much longer in Seattle than he had in Duluth; he was arrested by King County sheriff's officers on November 22, 1964, only eight months after he had arrived in Seattle. This time, the charge was second-degree burglary. On April 20, 1965, he was sentenced to serve fifteen years in the Washington state penal system. He was sent to the maximum-security prison in Walla Walla.

Locked inside the walls of the penitentiary located in the center of Washington's wheat country, Harvey availed himself of the opportunity to further his education. He obtained his high-school diploma, and then continued to study. He took many courses in sociology and psychology—college-level courses. He proved to be a most adept student, and his papers submitted on the sexual psychopath, the paranoid personality, and the well-adjusted individual garnered A's. He read voraciously, and studied journalism. His superior intelligence impressed his instructors.

Once again, despite some disciplinary problems due to his violent temper, he earned "good time," and he was freed on parole in a little over four years. He returned to Seattle.

Harvey was now forty-one years old, and, of course, still single. The nubile girl was the female who attracted him. He was fixated on the teenage girl as his ultimate sexual choice. That might seem obvious, since he had never had the opportunity to date girls when he himself was a teenager. He had emerged from prison a middle-aged man much marked by his experiences, and it was unlikely that any teenage girl would choose to date him. Therefore, he courted—and married— Sheila Moran, a divorcée with children. Sheila had her own home in Ballard, Seattle's Scandinavian district, and Harvey moved in with her after their marriage in 1969.

The marriage was doomed from the very beginning. Sheila was aghast at the motley crew of ex-cons who dropped in at all hours of the day and night. And she was annoyed that Harvey always had her car. He put more miles on the car in a year than she had in five. She would awake at night to find that Harvey was gone. He seemed to drive all night long, but he would never tell her what he was doing or where he had been when he returned. His standard reply was always, "I just had to get out and think."

What he thought about or why his thoughts were so oppressive that he had to drive a hundred miles or more to ventilate them was unclear to her.

"Harvey," she argued, "you have to be up to no good if you're just out there driving around aimlessly."

He would not respond. Her questioning irritated him, and he clammed up when confronted.

Rarely, he took Sheila with him on trips, but twice she went with him to Vancouver, British Columbia. One of Harvey's uncles lived there. The first time they journeyed into Canada, they were unable to locate the uncle, but the second trip was more successful. They brought the uncle back to Seattle for a visit. It was not the most propitious of family reunions.

Within a day of their return from Canada, they were sitting around making small talk when Harvey suddenly jumped upon his elderly uncle and beat him severely while Sheila watched in horror. Later, thinking that she should protect Harvey's uncle, she told the older man that she was going to report the beating to police. Although he was a mass of bruises and cuts and could barely hobble around, he insisted that if Sheila called the police, he would deny that the beating had occurred. "Leave him be."

Bewildered, Sheila kept her peace.

The marriage was interrupted when Harvey was arrested and sent to Walla Walla for parole violation and suspicion of robbery.

Harvey was in and out of Walla Walla in less than a year. He returned to Sheila and the children.

Sheila waited for an opportunity to be free of this violent man she had married, but before she could leave peacefully, there was a scene in which Harvey went berserk. She was sure that this time he was going to beat *her* to death. She managed to avert a beating by remaining calm, but she was terrified of him from then on.

When Harvey speaks of this first marriage, he claims that he cannot understand why it ended. He was working two jobs—by his reckoning—one as a construction worker during the day, and the other as a musician playing gigs at night. He does not mention the burglary and prostitution activities that King County sheriff's detectives felt he was deeply involved in.

"That marriage just went all to pieces," Harvey recalls. "I don't know why. I was working two jobs, and I was always trying to work around the house, and my wife didn't think I made enough money. So I took another job on the weekends at home—for the National Broadcasting Company. I was a carpenter, and I was making doors at this time that they could put on a sorority house and make it look like a Russian consulate, because they were making a movie over there.

"She [his wife] asked me if she could take the kids swimming, and I said, 'No. You had better stay because I have got a rush job, and I would have to have you run and get things,' and I went into the house to get her, and nobody was there. So about five hours later, they came home in the camper, and I was mad and I told her I didn't want any supper.

"So I came in in about an hour and asked if she would

make me a sandwich, and she said, 'You didn't want to eat then, and I am not feeding you now,' or something like that, and I got really mad. As a matter of fact, I go so mad, I don't remember part of it. When I looked up, her and the kids were running out of the house, and my head hurt real bad, so bad I never felt anything like it. I was seeing red in my eyes, and things shooting out.

"So in the kitchen, I had built a big breakfast bar, and on this side of it, we had stools—like they have in a bar, with soft padding you lean back on. I went in and sat and I turned away with my back to it. I closed my eyes and I saw God, and he told me to kill her. . . ."

Harvey had expected Sheila would be a softer, sweeter woman. He hadn't managed to marry a teenager, but he at least thought he had married a woman who would make him the most important thing in her life, cater to him, and understand him. Sheila's attitude was a crushing disappointment. She certainly hadn't been his first choice, but he was enraged to find that he had gotten himself a grown female who was as dictatorial and unyielding as the women who had controlled him when he was a child.

He walked down the basement steps and found a hammer. His wife and her children had not come back, and so he waited all night in the basement.

"I hid behind the furnace, and the next morning I heard steps upstairs. I came out from behind the furnace, and I heard steps coming down the stairs. So I waited beside the steps, and my stepdaughter who was seventeen—*she* came walking downstairs. I just looked at her, and I felt foolish. I thought it was my wife, and I was going to hit her. I didn't hit my stepdaughter because God hadn't told me to kill her. I would have hit my wife."

Harvey packed all his belongings into his pickup and drove off.

He did not return for six months. By that time the marriage was over for all intents and purposes. Sheila had seen a consuming rage in him, unlike anything she'd ever witnessed. He talked to her on the phone a few times. She agreed to meet with him, but only if friends accompanied them. She did not want him back, and he claims that he no longer wanted her.

He missed his stepdaughter sometimes; she had always been more his type than her mother was.

3

Harvey Carignan did not remain single long. In early 1972 he was forty-four years old, and bitter over the number of years of his life that had been swallowed up behind bars. He was not exactly what most women were looking for in a Prince Charming; he was actually an unattractive man; his hairline had fallen back from his peculiarly domed forehead, he had a receding chin and a deep scar over one eye. He looked years older than his true age, with his skin deeply lined, and bags and wrinkles beneath his eyes. His customary expression was still a glowering frown, and to smile, he had to make a concentrated effort.

But Harvey was a big, well-built man, and he affected sideburns that grew almost down to his dimpled chin. He could be charming when the occasion called for it, although he was also known for his occasionally blatant crudeness when he approached women. He could turn his charm off and on like a light switch.

He hid his temper well when he met Alice Johnson, and gave her the full impact of his charismatic persona. Alice was taken with him from the beginning. But then, Alice was a most vulnerable woman.

Alice Johnson had just been divorced too, and she found single life miserable. Like many newly divorced women, Alice needed proof that she was still attractive to men. If she should find someone else who cared for her enough to marry her, that would prove to her ex-husband that she was still a woman to be reckoned with.

Alice was a rather plain woman in her early thirties, but she had a trim figure and long brown hair to her shoulders. Even so, she was not deluged with invitations from men. Perhaps it was because she was not good at witty conversation. She was naive and gullible and her education had ceased when she finished the eighth grade. She worked cleaning houses, and occasionally cleaning furniture stores after business hours. As a cleaning woman, she had few opportunities to meet men. Her social life was worse than dull; it was almost nonexistent.

Alice started going to a small café just across the street from the Sav-Mor gas station, or to a neighborhood tavern—the Meet Me There tavern—which was next door to the café. And there in the tavern she did, indeed, meet someone: she met Harvey Carignan.

When she met Harvey, she was impressed. By this time he had managed to lease a Sav-Mor gas station from the Time Oil Company, and Alice thought he owned it. Business was brisk, and Harvey assured her it would get even better as gas shortages increased. She thought she had found herself a nice hardworking middle-aged man.

Alice owned her own home at 135th and 20th N.E., which Harvey moved into. Alice also had a son, Billy, eleven, and a daughter, Georgia, fourteen. Anybody who knew Harvey well could have told Alice that he never even glanced twice at attractive women in his own age bracket—that he was obsessed with teenage girls and that he often walked into restaurants and approached young girls with invitations and suggestions that were gross and embarrassing. Alice didn't even notice that Harvey seemed to favor Georgia over Billy.

When Alice and Harvey were married on April 14, 1972, the new bride really thought she had found herself a prize. He was smart, and he worked hard, and it was nice to have a man around the house again. Her family was not as entranced with Harvey, and her brother, particularly, looked upon him with suspicion.

The kids weren't crazy about their new stepfather either. He was a harsh disciplinarian and Alice's son was beaten severely several times. Her daughter, Georgia, had other reasons to feel anxious around Harvey; he looked at her sometimes in a way that didn't seem fatherly at all. Something about him made her shiver.

Just how much Alice knew about Harvey's past has never been established. She knew he'd had some trouble with the law, but she was easily convinced that the police had only been picking on him, making him the scapegoat for things he hadn't done. As far as she was concerned, he was a good husband. He took her on trips to Canada several times. She met his mother and stepfather in West Seattle, and Harvey talked of going back to Minnesota sometime so she could meet his half-brother and the rest of the family who lived there. Alice had her own car, and Harvey had several cars. Financially, they were living a very comfortable life.

Some second-wives-to-be make it a point to visit and talk with a man's first wife, and, in so doing, often come away with a whole different view of the man. Alice never considered doing that; she believed Harvey when he said that Sheila had been a nag who never appreciated anything he did. Even if she had attempted to consult with Sheila, it would have been an impossible task. Sheila was in hiding. She too was married again; she never wanted Harvey to know where she was. She'd seen his temper flare on that day when she'd taken her children swimming and she hoped devoutly that she would never see such blind anger again.

All wasn't perfection in Harvey's second marriage. Alice's son had had enough beatings, and he called his real father and told him that he wanted to live with him. Billy was out of the house within months of the marriage. Georgia would have liked to go too, but she worried about her mother and felt she should stay, confident that she could avoid Harvey's attentions.

Harvey did have a few eccentricities, but Alice figured that any man who had been single most of his life might be expected to be set in his ways. Harvey was a constant traveler. He put more miles on his vehicles than any man she'd ever known. Harvey had his yellow-and-black Chevrolet pick-up, a Pontiac Bonneville sedan, a 1968 Ford Torino, a 1963 Oldsmobile, and a purple Oldsmobile Toronado, and she had the tan 1967 Pontiac. Sometimes Harvey would take her along on his drives, but mostly he'd go alone, and she didn't know where he went.

Harvey was a fast driver, and he drove like the hounds of hell were after him. Alice didn't know that he'd gathered tickets like confetti, or that he ignored them. Between August 1969 and October 1972 he'd received seven tickets for speeding or for failure to stop. Harvey had been in the penitentiary for most of his adult life and unable to drive; not surprisingly, he didn't seem to demonstrate either skill or responsibility behind the wheel. He ignored edicts from the Department of Motor Vehicles and subsequently lost his license entirely.

Once the honeymoon period was over, Harvey turned out to be a less-than-perfect husband. When Alice angered him, he belted her across the face—and sometimes across the room. On one occasion it took five stitches to close the gash in Alice's lip. Another time, he blacked her eye, and she had to stay away from her family until the discoloration faded.

Alice did not consider this reason enough to end the marriage, however. She only vowed to be more careful in the future when she spoke to him, and tried not to nag or argue.

Georgia would have welcomed a divorce. She couldn't understand why her stepfather drove off so often at night. And he was always asking her to go for rides with him. On the few times when she could not avoid being in a car with him, she was terrified; the man drove eighty miles an hour on the freeway, darting in and out of traffic as if he were invincible.

One evening Harvey insisted that Georgia go for a ride with him, and there was no way she could get out of it. When they were safely away from the house, her stepfather suggested that she sit closer to him, as he wanted to have a talk with her. He explained that he was jealous when she had boyfriends, but only because he loved her so much; he was only taking a fatherly interest in her welfare. Georgia, much more aware than her mother was, did not find his hand on her leg a fatherly touch. She pleaded with him to turn the car around and take her back home, and he finally agreed.

Georgia felt uncomfortable around Harvey—even in her own home. He continued to stare at her so intently that she felt as if she were naked. One evening, when they were alone in the house, Harvey walked across the room toward her without saying a word. Still silent, he picked her up and began to carry her back toward the master bedroom. Georgia beat on her stepfather's shoulders and begged him to consider what he was doing. She asked him what her mother would think if she ever found out. Finally Georgia's words seemed to penetrate the blank stare on Harvey's face and he set her down. And apologized.

Not long after, Georgia ran away. She joined her brother and father in California.

Things seemed somewhat easier in the Carignan household once Alice's children were gone. She decided that it might be best after all if the youngsters stayed with their father until she and Harvey got their marriage on really solid ground.

4

On May 23, 1972, Kathy Sue Miller passed from her four-teenth year into her fifteenth—only a month after Harvey Carignan had married Alice Johnson. When Kathy became fifteen, Mary Miller heaved a figurative sigh of relief.

The nightmare had not come true.

Now Kathy Miller and Harvey Carignan lived in Seattle; indeed, they both lived in the north end of the Emerald City. There was no reason to foresee that they might ever meet. There are a million people living in the Seattle area.

On Tuesday, May 1, 1973, Kathy Miller happened to run her finger down a column of want ads in the Seattle *Times*'s evening edition. She pored over the classifieds, reading each ad in the help-wanted section. She wasn't looking for a job for herself, but for her boyfriend, Mark Walker. Mark had been looking for a part-time job, and Kathy was trying to help. She didn't need to find a job for herself, because she was pretty sure that she could find work as an aide in a nursing home. In fact, she already had a tentative appointment for the next day at a north-end convalescent home.

Mary Miller wasn't anxious for Kathy to take a job; there was enough money from Mary's job at the bank, and Kathy had opted to take a heavy class load at Roosevelt High School. She was getting excellent grades, and Mary thought it would be better if Kathy put off getting a job until the summer vacation.

And so, when Kathy circled a small ad on Tuesday night,

she did so only because the job looked like something Mark would like.

"Mom," she cried, "I think I've found a great job for Mark!"

Kathy went to the phone and dialed a number. Mary heard no conversation, and then Kathy sighed and hung up the phone.

"Nobody's there. The gas station must be closed. I'll try again in the morning."

At eight the next morning, Kathy tried the number again, and her mother could hear her talking to someone.

"How old do you have to be?" Kathy was asking. Then she exclaimed, "Oh . . . you take *girls*?"

Mary was in the next room, getting dressed to go to work, and she could hear her daughter answer "yes" and "no" to whatever questions the person on the other end of the line was apparently asking. She heard Kathy give her telephone number and address, and she frowned a little. She would have preferred that Kathy not give out specific information to a perfect stranger.

After about ten minutes, Kathy burst into the room. "Mom, he asked me all those questions. He practically interviewed me right on the phone!"

"What kind of a job is it?"

"A job in a gas station. He's going to pick me up in front of Sears after school at two-thirty and take me out to the station to fill out an application."

"Kathy, you don't know anything about cars or pumping gas, and I don't like you meeting a stranger. That isn't right. If you apply for a job, you should go yourself to the place of business. It might be dangerous getting in a car with a man you don't know anything about."

Kathy's reaction was that of a typical teenager. "Mom, you don't trust anybody."

"Don't you remember that girl I read about in the paper— the one who was picked up for some job, only it wasn't a real job? She was raped. I don't want you to go."

"Okay. I won't—but it sounds like it would be a good job."

"I mean it, Kathy. Don't even think about meeting him."

Kathy promised that she wouldn't, and Mary left the house to catch her bus. She walked to the corner to wait, but the whole conversation kept coming back to her. She wanted to be absolutely sure that Kathy understood the possible danger. Mary turned around and went back to talk to her daughter again; if she was late, she was late. This was more important than being on time for work.

Kathy listened impatiently as Mary stressed again that just because somebody had placed an ad in the paper, that didn't make him automatically all right. And Kathy promised again that she wouldn't go to meet the station owner.

Mary's bus had gone without her, and she and Kathy now rode the next bus together. Kathy got off first near Roosevelt High School, and Mary watched through the smudgy window as her beautiful daughter hurried away, turning once to wave happily.

Kathy had grown into a lovely young woman. She was tall, five feet, seven inches now, and weighed a hundred and forty pounds, a strong athletic girl. Her blond hair had darkened to a burnished butterscotch color and fell to the middle of her back in thick waves. Kathy had green eyes, and just the faintest suggestion of freckles sprinkling over her fair skin. She was very pretty, but she was hardly more than a child—unlike some teenagers, who are fifteen-going-on-forty. Kathy was shy, and much more attached to her family than most youngsters. She loved her brother, Kenny, and her black cats and white dog.

On that sunny May morning, Kathy wore a blue-and-white jumper that her Grandmother Purgalis had made for her, a navy-blue blouse, and blue-tinged nylons. She carried a suede purse and several schoolbooks as she walked toward the high school.

The bus sped up, and Mary could no longer see Kathy.

Mary was still anxious as the bus ascended the I-5 freeway ramp and hurtled south toward the downtown section of Seattle. She had asked Kathy questions during the short time they'd shared the bus ride. Did she know the man's name? No. Where was the gas station? She didn't know. What had the ad said? Only "service station help wanted" and a number with an LA prefix.

That hadn't seemed right to Mary. If the prefix was LA, the station would have been in the same neighborhood where they lived, someplace that Kathy could have reached easily on foot. She wouldn't have needed a ride from the owner.

During her morning's work, the job offer kept coming to Mary Miller's mind. The more she thought about it, the more nervous it made her. With a mother's sixth sense, she knew something was wrong. She had to go one step further to be sure Kathy was safe.

Mary dialed the Seattle Police Department and was put through to Sergeant Ed Golder, supervisor of the Sex Crimes Unit. She related the facts of the ad and Kathy's phone conversation, and asked Golder if it sounded peculiar to him.

"Yes," he answered. "That isn't the way it should be. Tell your daughter not to go. It could be all right, but it's always better to be cautious."

"I did tell her. That's exactly what I said—that she was not to go under any circumstances."

"Then it should be okay," Golder replied. "If there is any problem—if he calls her, or there's anything that worries you—feel free to call me."

Mary felt a little better after talking to the police sergeant, and thought perhaps she had worried particularly because she and Kathy were still concerned about the man who'd followed Kathy home from the swimming pool the week before. That was probably it—and it was ridiculous to think there could be any connection between the man at the pool and the man on the phone. Kathy had called the ad number purely by chance. And the man at the pool might only have been someone headed in the same direction as Kathy. Maybe Mary had warned Kathy too much, made her afraid of shadows. She supposed she would have to get used to men flirting with Kathy; she was so pretty, and she was growing up. With no father in the home, Mary had had to play both mother and father, and it had made her doubly vigilant.

Well, what of it? She was protective, and that was that.

Kathy wasn't home when Mary arrived in the late afternoon. She wasn't particularly concerned because she knew Kathy had thought about going out to the Columbia Lutheran Home to see about the aide job after school. It was still light outside and would be for a few more hours.

Everything seemed normal.

But time passed, and there was no greeting shout from Kathy as she came through the front door. Kenny kept asking where Kathy was, and by six Mary felt the first niggling of fear. The anxiety of the morning returned. She had to concentrate hard to allay the little darts of fear that made her hands shake.

By six-thirty Mary was drawn to the newspaper Kathy had left on the floor the night before. She turned to the classified section and looked for the ad about the gas-station job. But the ad wasn't there. There was only a hole in the paper where Kathy had torn it out.

Mary sent Kenny across the street to borrow last night's *Times* from the neighbors. She scanned the ads and found only one service-station job listed that included an LA number. Mary carried the paper to the phone and dialed the number given.

A man answered.

"Did you advertise for a job in last night's paper?" Mary asked.

"Yes."

"Did you happen to talk to a girl named Kathy Miller this morning?"

"Yes, I did. Just a minute, I'll get her slip."

Mary heard a female voice in the background, and then the man came back on the line and repeated Mary's own phone number to her. "Kathy Miller. Yes, she was supposed to come to the station at two-forty-five this afternoon, but she didn't show up."

Mary hung up. The man had seemed cooperative, but she was still worried. Kathy had not really disobeyed her; she had promised that she wouldn't get in a car with a strange man. Maybe she had decided to fudge on her promise a little, and had taken the bus out to the service station. Or walked. No, the man had said the station was located near 75th and Aurora. That was much too far for Kathy to walk.

How had Kathy known where the station was? She hadn't known in the morning. Maybe she'd called the man back and gotten the address. If that was true, why hadn't he mentioned that he'd talked to Kathy twice? He'd only said he'd talked to her in the morning.

More worrisome still, why hadn't Kathy appeared for the two-forty-five appointment? And where was she now?

Mary dialed the phone again. She called Kathy's best friend.

"Lisa," Mary asked, "was Kathy in school today? Did you see her at lunch?"

"I didn't eat lunch with Kathy today, but I saw her at school. She probably went to the library to study at noon—but she definitely was in school," the girl answered.

Mary called Mark Walker next, but Mark wasn't home; he was out for the evening at a Junior Achievement meeting. Then she called another of Kathy's girlfriends, and found that that girl was out too.

It was eight o'clock now, and the shadows outside had turned from golden to purple. Kathy hadn't come home for supper, and she hadn't called. She always called if she expected to be even fifteen minutes late.

Something was wrong.

Mary could wait no longer. She dialed 911, the Seattle police and fire emergency number. She told the operator who answered that she feared something had happened to her daughter.

Was it an emergency? Yes. *Yes!* But how could Mary convey to this disembodied voice on the phone that this was Kathy, this was a girl who was *always* home when she said she would be? The operator took down Mary's name and address and promised to send a patrol car by as soon as one was available.

At nine P.M. a two-man car out of the Wallingford precinct pulled up and Mary explained the circumstances to the patrolmen.

"I want you to check and find out where that LA number is. I called it, and a man answered and said Kathy was supposed to have come there today, but she didn't show up. He told me the station was at Seventy-fifth and Aurora, but I've looked through the phone book and I can't find any station listed in that location."

The officers promised that they would try to locate the station, but said they might not be able to trace the phone number until the next morning because it was difficult to obtain such traces after working hours at the phone-company offices. They could sense this mother's concern, but they were not as worried. The girl was almost sixteen, and it was only nine in the evening, hardly dark yet. They knew that most teenagers break their patterns once in a while. The girl could have met a friend, gone to a movie; there could be a dozen happy reasons why she was late.

At ten P.M. Mary called Mark Walker again.

"Mark, have you seen Kathy? She hasn't been home from school. Were you with her after school today?"

"Yes," the boy said slowly. "She was going to apply for a job. Some man was supposed to pick her up in front of Sears at two-thirty—"

"*What* man?"

And then Mary's worst fears seemed to have come true. "What man, Mark?"

"I don't know what his name was. He owns a gas station, and he was supposed to pick her up in a purple car."

"Did you see him? Did she go with him?"

"I don't know. I waited there on the corner with her for as long as I could, and I would have gone with her, but I had my paper route. When he didn't show up in ten minutes, I had to leave."

Her fingers trembling, Mary dialed 911 again. She felt she had vital information now, but the operator told her that she would have to wait until the Juvenile detectives came on at a quarter to eight the next morning.

Determined to find help immediately, Mary called the Wallingford precinct and asked for a car to come back to her house. About forty-five minutes later, another police officer came to her home. He took a report and promised to try to check out the number listed in the ad.

"But I may not be able to find out anything until morning," he warned—just as the other officers had. "The phone company's offices aren't open this time of night."

None of the officers reported back that night. Mary paced the floor all night long, hoping against hope that there was a reason that Kathy hadn't come home, a reason other than the awful pictures in her mind.

In the morning, Mary called the Juvenile Unit and talked to Detective Marilyn McLaughlin. McLaughlin said that she would track down the original reports and check out the unlisted phone number. At eleven McLaughlin called Mary and said that the number had been assigned to a business at 7216 Aurora Avenue North.

"The owner's name is Harvey Carignan."

Although Mary had spoken to the owner at the station the evening before, Harvey Carignan was not at the Sav-Mor when Marilyn McLaughlin arrived there. Business was proceeding as usual, and the attendants on duty on Thursday morning said they had never seen a girl who resembled Kathy Miller. None of them knew where their boss was.

Carignan did not appear for work during the day, nor could he be reached at his north-end home. When the four-to-twelve second-watch shift came on duty, one car was dispatched to Harvey's home and one car drove to the station. Harvey was located at his home, and he agreed to meet with the officers waiting at the station. He seemed cooperative, quite willing to discuss the matter of Kathy Miller, but he shrugged as he said he couldn't see how he could be of much help.

"This girl—this Kathy Miller—she was supposed to come out yesterday afternoon, but she never showed up."

The investigating patrol officers spoke with a young woman, Candy Erling, who worked at the station. She thought she might have seen Kathy.

"There *was* a girl here, only she was here today—not

yesterday. She came here in a white Chevrolet, and there was another girl and a guy about nineteen with long hair with her. She was here at three, and she said she needed a job to get money to go to California.''

"What was her name?''

"I don't know. I told her the boss wasn't here and she'd have to come back when he was.''

Candy couldn't remember what the girl had worn.

This information was relayed to Mary Miller, and she assured the policemen that Kathy didn't know anyone with a white Chevrolet. "And she didn't want to go to California. We talked about going to New Hampshire this summer to see one of her grandmothers—but not California. If she had wanted to go to California, all she would have had to do was call her uncles down there, and they would have bought her a plane ticket. That couldn't have been Kathy at the station.''

Up to this point, Kathy had been considered a runaway. Now that the arbitrary twenty-four-hour mark had been passed—the period set by most police departments before they officially declared an individual a missing person—Kathy's name was listed under that category.

"She's not missing because she wants to be,'' Mary said firmly. "Something's happened to her or someone is holding her against her will. We have to find her right away.''

Mary had expected that the police would now go into Harvey Carignan's gas station and home and search for Kathy. She did not know they were forbidden by the Constitution to do that. They had questioned the man she distrusted so, but that was all they could do. There was no evidence at all to support the contention that Kathy had actually met with Harvey Carignan—only Kathy's boyfriend's report that she had intended to apply for a job at his service station. That wasn't enough to constitute probable cause, which would allow them to go in and rip the man's property apart.

Mary Miller's sister drove slowly by the service station on Aurora and noted two cars there—one a maroon (or purple) Pontiac, and the other a car that looked to be white over maroon. She took the license numbers.

Detective McLaughlin ran the license numbers through the Department of Motor Vehicles in the state capital at Olympia. They came back registered to Harvey and his wife, Alice Carignan. McLaughlin next put in a request for any rap sheet that might be extant on Harvey Louis Carignan.

In the meantime, Mary was attempting to do detective work on her own. Through bank channels she was able to do a credit check on Carignan. He came back clean. Whatever he had done, he had not gotten into financial difficulties recently. It didn't help much to know that. It didn't help at all.

Mary felt immensely frustrated when it seemed there was no legal way to force the man to tell the truth, a truth she was sure he was concealing. When she and her sister and brother-in-law drove by the Sav-Mor again, he was not around. Nor were any vehicles parked in front of his home. Had she been able to locate Harvey Carignan, Mary herself would have throttled the truth out of him. Anything to find Kathy before it was too late.

Mary called contacts her family had established over the years, the FBI, the chief investigator for the Boeing Airplane Company, and she called the papers—everyone and anyone who might help her break through the system.

And then, late on this second day, she took pictures of Kathy into Detective McLaughlin, and a small square of fabric, the blue-and-white cloth left after Mrs. Purgalis had finished making the jumper Kathy had worn. The last glimpse Mary had had of Kathy burned in her mind. Her smiling daughter, dressed in the jumper, walking away from the bus toward her school.

Kathy was gone. Simply gone, swallowed up in a city with half a million people, perhaps into a county with another half-million, or perhaps even farther away. There seemed to be no way at all to find her.

Mary tried not to think of her nightmare, the dream that was now fifteen years old. And yet it clung to her, flashing across her mind whenever she could not block it.

She spent another night without sleep.

On Friday morning, May 4, Mary received a call from detectives in the Homicide Unit. Kathy's case had been assigned to that division, and that could only mean that they now believed that her daughter had met with foul play.

The nightmare accelerated.

5

On that Friday morning, May 4, 1973, Kathy Miller had been missing more than forty-one hours. For the first twenty-four hours she had been thought to be a runaway. For the next sixteen, she had been listed officially as a missing person. Hindsight is always keener than trying to guess at the future, and it seems clear now that Kathy should have been considered a victim of foul play from the very beginning. For Juvenile detectives—who have dealt with thousands of teenage girls who run away for a day or so—the twenty-four-hour-wait rule suffices in almost all cases. However, confrontations with Harvey Carignan and interviews with Kathy's mother kept pointing to tragedy.

When the case was transferred to the Homicide Unit early Friday morning, police officials were almost certain that Kathy was either dead or held captive somewhere. They would have liked to believe the latter, but sad experience told them that that was probably false optimism. It is a moot point today whether an all-out search would have found Kathy on the evening she disappeared. Probably not. It is clear, though, that there might have been physical evidence still available that could have closed the case cleanly years ago.

By the luck of the draw, the next detectives up for major case assignment were Billy Baughman and Duane Homan. Homicide detectives always work in teams—for pragmatic reasons. At a crime scene, two pairs of hands are essential: to gather and label evidence, to take pictures, to hold either end of a tape measure to chart the scene so that it can be reestablished absolutely long after the body is removed. And, more than that, two men—totally in tune with each other—can toss ideas back and forth and evaluate theories in an attempt to solve what sometimes seems, initially, unsolvable.

In 1973, there were seven homicide teams, three sergeants, a lieutenant, and a captain working crimes-against-persons in the Seattle Police Department. The teams were always referred to as if the detectives were literally joined at the hip with their partners: Reed-and-Dorman, Fonis-and-Cameron, Moran-and-Miller, Baughman-and-Homan, their names run together when they were spoken.

All in all, fourteen detectives selected to be partners for almost ephemeral reasons, but for reasons that worked.

Billy Baughman and Duane Homan are both solidly built men who stand well over six feet tall, and they both have brown hair. In one case, when they were searching for a missing five-year-old girl, they worked on it so diligently that they became familiar fixtures in the missing child's home. The victim's younger brother could never distinguish between them and addressed both of them as "Boman."

They were both in their mid-thirties in 1973, and both detectives had been in Homicide for several years, after working their way up through the ranks. They were, and continue to be, excellent investigators. While Baughman is expansive and something of a joker, Homan tends to be more reflective. They made a solid team and they worked together with precision—two detectives that no killer would care to have walking behind him.

Harvey Carignan would shortly develop an abiding hatred for Billy Baughman and Duane Homan.

The Kathy Miller case would haunt Baughman and Homan forever. Each man had a teenage daughter at the time they were given the Miller case. When Duane Homan looked at the pictures that Mary Miller had provided, his breath caught and his stomach convulsed; Kathy looked so much like his own daughter that she might have been a twin.

The two detectives read through the information that had accumulated since Mary Miller's first call. Kathy had apparently intended to meet Carignan on a busy street corner in the

Roosevelt district at two-thirty on the previous Wednesday afternoon. She had never come home, and Carignan had steadfastly denied any contact with her at all—beyond a phone call. The patrol officers who had talked to him were not sure if the man had lied; he seemed to be a normal businessman, and he was married. Not the prime suspect for kidnap and whatever else might have occurred. But then, both investigators knew that when you deal with homicides, things are seldom what they seem—that most killers have black, hidden sides to their personalities.

Had it been up to Homan and Baughman, they would have pulled all the stops within minutes of Mary Miller's first call to 911. Their orientation is in the investigation of violent deaths. Homicide men are trained to expect the worst: each death they probe is looked at first as a possible murder, next as a possible suicide, third as an accident, and only then as a death by natural causes. Homicide detectives are the pessimists of police work; they have to be. By always expecting murder, they can be sure they will not lose physical evidence or good witnesses. If evidence is not retrieved at once from a crime scene, it may well be lost forever. Witnesses tend to scatter—or to forget vital information. A crime scene has to be worked meticulously on the first go-round.

In this case, they wanted mightily to find some happy reason why Kathy Miller had not come home, but when they looked at Harvey Carignan's rap sheet, their hearts sank. The suspect had been convicted of murder twenty-three years earlier, and had had the conviction reversed on a technicality. And that murder appeared to have been the result of a thwarted rape. There were three other arrests listed for sexual assault, and several for burglary. This man had spent most of his adult life in prison, and the rest of it on parole.

And this was the person whom Kathy had gone off to meet. . . .

Baughman and Homan drove to the bank where Mary Miller worked so that they might interview her. She explained that she couldn't bear to stay home and wait, that every phone call made her jump with a mixture of anticipation and dread. Work provided little salvation, but it helped to pass the hours.

The detectives saw a very slim blond woman, her thick hair pulled into a chignon. Her hands trembled as she lit a cigarette and tried to recall everything she could for them.

"I remember that she talked to that man for more than ten minutes. I heard her laughing as if someone on the other end of the line was making jokes. From the tone of her voice, I thought it was probably one of her friends. When she hung up, she was so excited. She kept saying, 'He practically interviewed me right on the phone!' She was convinced she could get the job. And I kept warning her not to go, that it didn't seem right to me."

Mary Miller thought—like any layman whose child has vanished—that the detectives could now go out and search Harvey Carignan's property, that they could arrest him. She could tell that they presumed Kathy had met with foul play. Wouldn't that mean that they could search? Wouldn't that mean arrest? They had to explain to her that it didn't. They had no probable cause, nothing concrete beyond the fact that Kathy had talked to the man on the phone the day she disappeared.

The detectives made a list of Kathy's friends' addresses, the names of her relatives, all of the other places she had applied for jobs, or intended to apply.

"Where is Kathy's father?" Homan asked. "Is it possible that she would have gone to see him or that he might have taken her away?"

Mary shook her head. "No. He hasn't seen the children since Kathy was three. I believe he's in the Salt Lake City area, but I'm positive he couldn't be involved in this."

The detectives tried to reassure Kathy's mother, but it was heavy work. "We'll be in touch with you constantly. When we go off duty, other detectives will take over."

Billy Baughman handed Mary a card with the number of the Homicide Unit.

Next the detective pair visited the parole officer who had most recently dealt with Carignan. He pulled Carignan's files and nodded. "He was under my supervision for a short time in

1971. He was in Walla Walla in the sixties—went up for burglary: fifteen years. He was paroled on August 12, 1968. His parole was subsequently revoked on June 30, 1970, and he was back in the joint until February 16, 1971. He continued on parole until July 28, 1972. Since then, he's been on inactive parole: all that means is that he is required to write a letter once a year and report how he's doing.''

"What was your impression of him?'' Homan asked.

"He seemed straight, but I found out he had periods of extreme violence. His wife—his ex-wife—was terrified of him. Once, in the penitentiary, he beat up a guard, and it took six guards to control him. He spent a year in 'the hole' for that. When things are going right, Harvey's a pretty decent person, but when things aren't going right, he turns into an animal. If you have to arrest him, he'll be dangerous; he won't go easy.''

When Homan and Baughman went off duty, Detectives Dick Reed and Wayne Dorman took over for the weekend. They touched base first with Mary Miller and let her know they would be in the field looking for Kathy but that she could reach them by calling Radio. Their impression was the same as every other officer's had been: here was a mother who had had a close bond with her daughter.

Reed and Dorman drove to the Sav-Mor station and noted that neither Carignan's car nor his wife's was parked there, and they next found that there were no vehicles outside the Carignan residence in the north end. The curtains were closed, and there was no activity around the place. It appeared that the Carignans had taken a trip.

Next the detectives went to the corner of 65th N.E. and Roosevelt—the last place Kathy had been seen. They canvassed every business in the area, asking if anyone remembered a tall, shy girl dressed in blue. No one did. Kathy must have gotten into a car willingly. If she had fought or screamed, surely someone in the busy area would have noticed a commotion.

Reed and Dorman checked Ravenna and Cowan parks, great forested areas close to the Roosevelt district. They knew that they were looking for a body, although neither of them acknowledged that grim fact aloud. Instead, they walked slowly through the wooded parks, poking into piles of brush and working far back into the shadows of the densest thickets. They were vastly relieved when their sweep of the parks netted nothing.

They visited the Wallingford precinct substation and passed out pictures of Kathy Miller to the officers on duty. Now every patrol car in the north end was looking for Kathy. Patrolmen watched for tall, blond girls, and they saw many—but when they looked more closely, they could see that the girls didn't really resemble the girl in the pictures they carried.

Dick Reed and Wayne Dorman made another pass by the gas station and Carignan's home, and found that he had not returned.

When Homan and Baughman returned to work at seven-thirty on Monday morning, Kathy had been missing five days. A confrontation with the suspect would have to be handled very, very carefully; the detectives had read about how he had avoided the gallows on a technicality more than two decades before. Any evidence obtained without probable cause would be considered in court "fruit of the poisoned tree"—evidence obtained illegally, and therefore tainted and inadmissible. What Homan and Baughman needed was that probable cause to obtain a search warrant, and they did not yet have it.

Without a body, or blood, or anything to indicate that Kathy had met with foul play, Harvey was as innocent as a lamb, and Harvey knew the rules. He had won before.

They talked with Mark Walker, the boy who had walked Kathy to the corner in front of Sears on May 2.

"I met Kathy at two-thirty-five P.M.—just by accident, because she doesn't usually walk that way. I asked her why she was going that way, and she told me she found the job wanting service-station help in the want-ads. She said she thought it would be a job for me and she called the number, and the man told her he wanted girls 'cause he already had boys working for him. She was going to apply for the job. I asked her where the service station was, and she said she didn't know—that the guy was picking her up in front of

Sears in a purple or wine-colored car. I questioned her about meeting a guy on a street corner to apply for a job. I said that was very unbusinesslike to meet a job applicant like that. She said the guy sounded okay over the phone.''

Mark looked down at his hands, and his voice was choked as he continued. "I told her maybe he was going to pick her up for something other than a job interview. Gee, we both chuckled about it, and shrugged it off.''

Mark explained that he'd had to leave at ten minutes to three, and that neither of them had seen a wine-colored car. "I left her there alone.''

"Can you remember what Kathy had on that day?'' Homan asked.

"Yes. Blue jumper, blouse, stockings, a waist-length gray jacket. She had an orange plastic notebook, a robin's-egg-blue notebook, and one schoolbook—but I don't remember which it was. She had a brown purse with a shoulder strap. It had metal chain links holding the strap to the purse.''

"Was Kathy happy at home?''

"Yes. Absolutely. She wouldn't have run away. She didn't drink, and she never touched drugs. She was—is—shy, but she has a lot of friends.''

And so the probe continued, beginning always with those closest to the alleged victim, asking questions, comparing answers—and then spreading out farther and farther.

The man that detectives really wanted to query closely was, of course, Harvey Carignan. And yet they feared "spooking" him, and they wanted to avoid that. He was watched covertly, and he continued to follow his normal patterns. When stakeout detectives drove past the Carignan home on Monday afternoon at two-thirty, the drapes were still pulled, but the purplish Toronado was parked in front. They did not stop, but only noted the information.

The decision was made to inform the media of Kathy's disappearance, and her picture and description appeared in late Monday and early Tuesday editions of the local papers. Along with a description of Kathy's clothing, the schoolbook and notebooks were mentioned and a request was made that anyone having information about Kathy should contact Homan or Baughman in the Homicide Unit.

A call came early Tuesday morning—not to detectives but to Mary Miller. Her phone number was not listed in the telephone directory. The caller had found the number written in the front of a schoolbook. The caller's only intention was to return the books to the owner, and he had no idea of the import of his call to Mary Miller.

"We have your daughter's books—her algebra book," the caller said.

"Where are you?" Mary asked. "Where did you find her things?"

The caller explained that he was a timekeeper at a business in Everett, some twenty-six miles north of Seattle. The books had been found in the parking lot of the Everett Plywood Company, a retail firm. Mary immediately called Billy Baughman and Duane Homan, who had just come on duty, and told them of the find.

The detectives left at once for Everett, where the time-keeper of the firm said that the books had been found on Thursday, May 3, at four A.M., on a ledge abutting the company's parking lot by one of the employees reporting for work. There were an algebra book, a German book, and a social-security card in the name of Kathy Miller.

"We had a group of schoolchildren touring through here on Wednesday," the timekeeper said, "and we assumed one of them had set the books down and forgotten them. We tried all day Thursday to locate the owner. Then I thought I'd try calling the number I found written in the algebra book. I called and got the mother. Until then, I didn't realize that the girl was missing."

"Then you didn't see who left the books there?"

The man shook his head. The books had been found after the school tour had left. He didn't remember any vehicles that had seemed suspicious, but then, there was a lot of traffic coming and going at the firm, and no one took special note of cars in the lot.

The plywood firm's parking lot abutted railroad tracks, and there were boxcars waiting for loading on the tracks. Homan and Baughman crawled into all those boxcars and searched the dark corners inside, thinking that at any moment they would find Kathy. But she wasn't there.

Next they clambered over huge stacks of rough logs piled nearby. A body could have been secreted in the crevices between the jumble of fir trees, and no one would find it for a long time. Billy Baughman, intent on the search, missed his footing and fell heavily from atop the tall stack of logs. He heard a sharp crack, and felt a stab of pain in his ankle. He ignored the discomfort, and kept searching.

By the time the detectives were satisfied that Kathy's body was nowhere in the area of the plywood mill and had returned to Seattle, Baughman's ankle had swollen to three times its normal size. It was broken.

Impatiently he had it cast, and continued on the case.

The discovery of Kathy's schoolbooks in Everett had told the detectives one thing at least: someone had taken Kathy—or her possessions—a long way away from the corner of 65th and Roosevelt.

Early the next morning the detective team drove past the Carignan home and saw that the pickup truck registered to Harvey was there. The front bumper appeared to be "dinged up," and white paint had been spattered over it.

Once Kathy's picture had been published in the paper and flashed across television screens, the calls began to pour in. A log was set up in Homicide, and each call was noted. Every one of the tipsters was convinced that he had seen Kathy: hitchhiking . . . sitting in a restaurant . . . arguing with a boyfriend . . . walking along a highway . . . at the Apple Blossom Festival in Wenatchee, Washington . . . walking aimlessly along a West Seattle street without a coat against the rain.

All of the informants were sure that the girl they had seen looked just like the picture of Kathy. Some of the tips were obviously off the wall, and some sounded possible. The possibles were followed up, and ended, always, in disappointment. There were so many pretty teenagers with long blond hair, but none of them was Kathy.

One report was frightening. A woman who lived in the

north Seattle suburb of Edmonds said she'd received a phone call about two A.M. Saturday that had awakened her from a sound sleep.

"The man on the line said he'd picked up a girl about twelve who was hitchhiking. He told me that he was allowing the girl one phone call for help, that he was permitting that one phone call because he'd been under psychiatric care and he didn't want to do anything to hurt her, but he was afraid he might. I dropped the phone because I was still half-asleep and because the call frightened me. When I picked it up, the line had gone dead."

A sick obscene call—but nothing to do with Kathy Miller. At five feet, seven inches tall, no one could have mistaken Kathy for a twelve-year-old.

There were a lot of calls from mentally unbalanced people, those designated "220's" in Seattle police lingo, deranged and occasionally sadistic people who come out of the woodwork when a case is highly publicized.

One caller claimed that he was holding Kathy Sue Miller and would release her only if thirty-six thousand dollars in unmarked bills was left at a place he would designate in his next call. He never called back.

A motorist called to say he'd picked up a young male hitchhiker who had run out of gas. "He kept talking about the girl whose picture was in the paper. He said that he could see why someone would want to rape and kill a girl as pretty as that. I told him I didn't want to continue in that vein of conversation. But I decided to find out something about him. He said his name was Howard and he said he went to school at Everett Community College. He mentioned that 'Sue' Miller's books were found only a mile from his parents' home. But he would never tell me his last name or his address. He asked to be let out in the university district in Seattle, and I was glad to have him out of the car. But then . . . I got to thinking . . ."

By the end of May, the log of calls would include more than a hundred tips, few of them useful. Most of the callers had only wanted to help, some of them were clearly deranged, and some of them probably only sought the two-thousand-dollar reward Kathy's grandparents were offering.

One young woman called and said that she had applied for a job at Harvey Carignan's gas station. The pretty twenty-year-old told detectives that she had gone to the Sav-Mor station at the end of April, and again on the first day of May. She told the detectives that she'd found Harvey less than professional and that she'd wondered why he'd advertised when he didn't even have a vacancy.

"I was hired twice, but I never worked there. First, he told me he didn't have the heart to fire the girl who was working there in April. Then he called me and asked me to come in again. When I got there, he told me I was hired, but then he said he had another reason for calling me; he wanted to take me out to dinner. I told him I wasn't interested. He told me I could stop by anyway and he'd give me a free tank of gas. I did go and get the gas, and he was a perfect gentleman; he didn't mention a date again."

It was becoming apparent that Harvey was not the world's most faithful husband. Another woman called after seeing Harvey mentioned in the papers as a possible suspect in Kathy's disappearance.

"I bought two tires from him. I paid twenty-five dollars down, and I was to pay the next twenty-five in a month. When I got the tires, he asked me if I'd like to get both tires for only twenty-five dollars. I asked him what the catch was, and he just grinned and said I knew what it was. I declined his offer, and I paid the whole fifty dollars—but I took his offer as a definite proposition."

And with all the calls from the public—most of them useless—there were the expected "urgent" messages from psychics or would-be psychics. One woman said that she had received a call from a seer in Florida who had "seen" Kathy.

"She says that she can see the letters 'K.C.' and the name 'Cecil.' Her celestial reading shows that the girl is dead, but she wasn't murdered—she drowned. Her body is in seven feet of muddy water near the crew house at the University of Washington. There are bells or chimes playing in the background where she is. The body will float to the surface in one week. . .''

At this point, Kathy had vanished so completely that detectives would have been willing to listen to a psychic if she had good information, but the clairvoyants who contacted them were vague and completely off in their information.

Kathy's books had been found, but there was no chance of lifting any prints from the book covers. They had been wet from rain when the employee at the plywood firm found them, and he had wiped them dry, unknowingly obliterating any fingerprints that might have been there.

Working with the ninhydrin process, Criminalist Karl Jepsen *had* managed to raise some latent prints from pages inside the books, but he could not match them to Harvey Carignan's prints that were on file from his previous scrapes with the law.

Harvey himself was not anxious to talk to the police.

6

With the discovery of Kathy's schoolbooks twenty-six miles from where she had last been seen, Duane Homan and Billy Baughman were sure that she was dead. There had been no reason for Kathy—or her books—to be in Everett. The probe now would concentrate on tying the suspect, Carignan, to Kathy. And that meant that the time had come to talk with Harvey.

While Detective Roy Moran watched the station from a hidden vantage point to see if Harvey would bolt and run when a crew of investigators approached him, Sergeant Bruce Edmunds and Detectives Duane Homan and Dick Reed walked into the station.

Homan introduced himself and the other detectives and said, "We're working on the disappearance of Kathy Sue Miller—which you undoubtedly have heard about. You seem to have been one of the last people to talk to her. I'm going to advise you now of your rights under Miranda."

While Homan repeated the familiar cautions regarding the right to have an attorney, to remain silent, Harvey interrupted with a hurried explanation of his own whereabouts on May 2. He submitted that he could not have encountered Kathy Miller—he had been much too busy running his business and collecting auto parts for customers.

Undaunted, Homan continued until the Miranda card had been read.

"This young woman doesn't seem to us to be an ordinary runaway," he said to Carignan.

Harvey said he did recall that Mary Miller had contacted him concerning her daughter. "I told her that the girl had called on Wednesday morning looking for a job for her boyfriend. I set up an appointment for two-thirty that afternoon. I was out at that time, but my girl who works here said she did come in with two hippie-looking guys, and they didn't wait around."

"I thought you were supposed to pick her up that afternoon."

Carignan nodded his head. "Yes. She called me again that day during the noon hour and she told me she was interested in the job, as she needed money to go to California. I think we talked about fifteen minutes. I agreed to pick her up at two-thirty in front of Sears."

"Did you go over there?" Homan asked.

Harvey's face was dotted with sweat and seemed to twitch nervously. He finally said, "Well, yes. I did go over there."

"Which car did you drive?"

"My 1966 Oldsmobile Toronado. But she wasn't there. I'm a busy man and I can't wait around all day. I waited two or three minutes and then I left to pick up some auto parts."

"Who was the girl who said she saw Kathy?"

"That was Candy Erling. She worked for me for three or four days and then she quit. I rehired a fellow who worked for me before to replace her."

"Could we see Candy's employment application?"

"She never filled one out."

"No withholding or social security?"

Harvey perspired more profusely. "No. The type of people I get in here never stay long enough to bother with all that."

"Do you know where Candy lives?"

"No. I took her home a few times, but it was always to a different place. Maybe she lives out near 175th and Aurora, but I took her and dropped her off at the A & P store once, too."

"You never asked her why she 'lived' in so many different locations?"

"It wasn't my business. I figured she was staying with different girlfriends or something."

"Do you ever loan your car to anyone?" Homan asked.

"Sometimes to customers, sometimes to kids who work here."

"Did you loan it to anyone Wednesday or Thursday last week?"

"No. I don't think so. I usually drive my truck, though."

"Did you drive it last week?"

"No. It was being repaired. A friend of mine towed it from my house to work on it at his station."

"You say you never saw Kathy . . . in person?"

"I never did."

"Would you be willing to take a polygraph about this matter?"

"I would."

The detectives stopped the conversation and walked out of the office, and Harvey trailed after them.

"If I took the lie-detector test and passed, would I be eliminated as a suspect?"

"Yes."

"What if I didn't pass it?"

"Then we'd be more concerned about you, Harvey, and the investigation would probably bear down in your direction," Homan responded.

"I'll talk to my lawyer about it and let you know."

Harvey was nervous, and seemingly a lot more nervous than an innocent man questioned by the police might be. The detective team thought it peculiar that he hired and fired so many young women at his station. They set out to locate Candy Erling, whose employment had ended precipitately right after she had given Harvey an alibi by insisting that Kathy *had* come to the service station the day after the afternoon she had vanished.

At this point the Seattle detectives even wondered if Candy might have disappeared mysteriously too. As it turned out, Candy, seventeen, was alive and well—but unemployed. She said she'd started to work at the Sav-Mor station on April 30, and left on the sixth of May.

"He fired me. He said that in the five days I worked, the till was short forty-seven dollars. I know I didn't take it, but

I've seen him dipping in there all the time to buy beer and food, and he never writes down what he takes out. The first day I was there he drank a half a case of beer, and he drank beer every other day too—only not as much as the first day.''

"How did you get the job?'' Billy Baughman asked.

"Through an ad in the Seattle *Times*. I phoned and asked if the job was still open. He wanted to know my age, if I was in school—which I'm not—and if I was married. I told him I was single, and he had me come down to the station. He didn't care that I had no experience in a station or with making change. He wanted to know how I'd get to work and I said I'd hitchhike or take a bus or have friends bring me. Then he asked if I could use a car, and he said he'd sell me one. I was supposed to get a dollar twenty-five an hour, and after I was trained, he would pay me a dollar sixty-five an hour and put thirty-five cents of that on the car. He never did tell me what the full price of the car was supposed to be.

"Then he started to tell me how ladylike I was, and how nice I looked and stuff. He reached for the collar of my backless dress and said 'nice material.' I told him to keep his hands to himself and he backed off. He liked that. He said, 'I like you. You are hired.' ''

Harvey had had other plans for Candy, however.

"He told me that what he said next would have no effect on my job, as I was hired already. He offered me twenty dollars' advance, and then he wanted to know if I had a boyfriend. I told him no, and he said he only asked because he didn't like kids hanging around the station. Then he asked me if I was a virgin, and I said no. He said he only asked that because if I really loved some guy, that would make me frustrated.''

Harvey next offered to give Candy the twenty-dollar advance and the car "*if* . . .''

"He said I knew that there was going to be an 'if,' and I said that I did. He then said '. . . *if* I can make love to you.' I said no. Then he said, 'How about when you get to know me better?' and I said no. He said I had a lot of guts and that he would drop it for the time being.''

Candy had the job, and Harvey had given her money to

take a bus home and change her clothing. She went to work that afternoon.

"He only brought sex up again one more time, and I said that I only wanted to make love with people my own age and that he should make love to people his age. He then told me that he had a lot of women who came into the station, and that he would fill up their gas tanks and then take them into the back room and have sex with them."

Asked about Harvey's activities on May 2, Candy recalled that he had left the station about two-twenty-five to go and get some auto parts. He expected to be back in half an hour.

"He called about forty-five minutes later and said he had to go to another auto-parts store, and it would be a while. He asked if I could handle the station and I said, 'Sure.' "

"When did he come back?"

"Between six-thirty and six-forty-five P.M. He didn't unload any auto parts."

"What was he wearing that day?" Homan said.

"He was wearing work-type green shirt and pants, military lace-up boots. His sleeves were rolled up and his pants were tucked into his boots."

Candy said she hadn't noticed anything unusual about her employer's demeanor that night. In fact, he had driven her home. She thought it was a little strange that he hadn't unloaded any auto parts and that she could see none in the back of the purple Toronado.

"He was very nervous the next day, after the police came to the station. Really jumpy. He told me the police try to get him for something every time he turns around."

Candy Erling was a worldly, savvy little teenager—the exact opposite of Kathy Miller. Candy had told Harvey to keep his hands off her, and he'd seemed to back off.

But shortly after that, he'd manufactured an excuse to fire her.

All the Seattle detectives had established at this point was that Harvey was an ex-con and a philanderer. His two-line ad in the paper assured him of a steady response from young women desperate for a job. They had no idea how many girls had answered the ad and been propositioned. More ominous, they had no idea how many girls might have vanished, just as Kathy had. There were so many teenagers on their own who had no mothers to report that they had never come home.

What the detectives did not yet have was a link between Kathy and Harvey beyond the fact that she had intended to meet with him on May 2.

Duane Homan and Billy Baughman contacted businesses near the Sav-Mor station to see if any of the owners or employees had seen or heard anything unusual on May 2 and subsequently. They located a young man, seventeen, who worked at the Texaco station across the street from Harvey's business. The youth said that he had been at work on May 2 around four P.M.

"I was talking with one of the guys there. I noticed a young girl about seventeen standing in the Sav-Mor station. She was wearing a blue outfit and had long, blond hair. She was really cute and I asked Bob if she was going to work at the Sav-Mor. He didn't know."

The witness was shown a picture of Kathy and he said she looked like the girl he'd seen except that that girl had had shorter hair which seemed lighter blond than the picture indicated.

This puzzled the investigators. If Kathy had been in Harvey's station on May 2, it would have been only for the briefest period since Candy Erling was positive Harvey hadn't come back on May 2 until after six P.M. No one else had seen the girl in the blue outfit. Was it possible that Harvey *had* brought Kathy to his station, and left before Candy had returned from pumping gas?

Possible, but not likely. Had it been Kathy's ghost? No, they'd been listening to too many psychics. Even less likely. The only reasonable explanation was that the witness had seen Kathy's picture in the papers and *imagined* that he'd seen her earlier.

Information elicited from the Texaco station owner was much more meaningful.

"I saw Harvey at seven A.M. on May 3 and he was getting out of his purple Toronado. He looked totally wasted, and I assumed he'd had another fight with his wife and slept in the car all night. He came over and asked me if I would fix his pickup truck as he couldn't get it running. He gave me the keys to the truck and I said I'd see what I could do. When he got out of his car, he had a blanket around his shoulders. He looked as if he hadn't slept all night—he had big dark circles under his eyes and his face was all dragged out.''

Where had Harvey been all night on May 2?

Alice Carignan was wondering the same thing, although she couldn't ask Harvey about it. She was worried. The police had come to their home, and they'd been to the Sav-Mor station twice to talk to Harvey. She had read all the articles in the newspapers about the missing girl, and now the papers were printing Harvey's name as the last person who was supposed to have seen Kathy Miller. She saw that her husband was very nervous. His face was twitching again.

She knew that Harvey hadn't been home all night on the day the girl was supposed to have vanished. She knew, because she'd waited up for him and he hadn't come back until after breakfast in the morning and he'd told her he had to get his truck fixed. He hadn't come home the next night either.

And then he'd asked her to take his Toronado to the car wash and have it washed. He'd been specific that he wanted her to vacuum the interior thoroughly at the car wash. She'd had it washed, all right, but she'd seen no need to vacuum it there when she had a perfectly good vacuum at home. So she'd taken it home to vacuum, but she hadn't told Harvey that. She'd lied and said she'd done exactly as he said. Now she was worried that he'd find out. She told her girlfriend what she'd done, but she didn't tell her husband.

Still, Alice couldn't believe that Harvey could have done anything wrong. The police were just looking for a patsy, and that explained why he was so nervous all the time. When she tried to talk to him, he just walked away from her and told her to shut up.

She noticed the cars driving slowly by their house, and she wondered if that was the police. She had half a mind to stop one of those cars and explain to them how kind Harvey really was, how hard he worked, and how good he was to her—at least most of the time.

Alice was being hounded too. Her family had never really taken to Harvey, and now her brother was suggesting that Harvey might be guilty of something awful. In fact, her brother said she should move out while she still could. Well, she wouldn't do that. She would stick by Harvey.

One of Harvey's friends was worried too. Harvey had come to him and explained that the police were trying to manufacture a case. Harvey needed an alibi.

Harvey had told him that he would explain what really happened on May 2.

"I killed two ex-cons that day. I had to stab one and shoot the other. I bloodied them up pretty good. I put them in the trunk of a car that's not traceable. I took them out in the woods to bury them, but while I was burying one, the other one got up and ran away."

Old Harv had really been bent out of shape about that deal. While he told the story, the sweat had just poured off his face, and he'd kept pulling at his cheeks like they were made out of Silly Putty. His friend wasn't about to alibi for Harvey because the story was just too weird. But he wasn't going to go to the police about it, either—not right away.

For one thing, Harv was a friend; for another, Harv was the strongest man he'd even seen in his life, and not a good guy to cross.

Harvey had gone next to one of his employees, a young man, and persuaded him to furnish the alibi. The employee told detectives that Harvey had been at the station at three-fifteen on May 2. This alibi witness wasn't a convincing liar, however, and Homan and Baughman already had Candy Erling's statement that Harvey had been gone for four hours— from two-twenty-five to six-thirty that day.

If Harvey was nervous—and he was—he had good reason to be. Police officials now assumed that he had disposed of Kathy Miller's body in some isolated region, and he was tailed constantly on the supposition that he might try to return to the body site to be sure he had hidden his victim completely.

Since he was known to have made frequent trips to Canada

in the past, it was possible that he had driven north to the border above Bellingham, Washington, crossed over into British Columbia, and secreted the body there.

Harvey was such a constant driver that the task of following him was not easy. *Air One*, the Seattle police helicopter, hovered over his pickup as he took off one morning. The pilot and observer were able to follow him as he drove to south Seattle—where he filled up his gas tanks in a service station on Empire Way—and then across the floating bridge toward the Snoqualmie Pass at the summit of the Cascade Mountains. That surveillance might have ended in tragedy; the helicopter developed mechanical trouble and had to set down at the summit. When it was airborne again, Harvey's truck had vanished.

Air One made several sweeps over the I-90 freeway, but they couldn't find their quarry. When they began to run out of gas, they turned the bird back toward Seattle.

Later in the day, a ground team spotted Harvey back at his home. If he had headed toward a body site high in the mountains, they had lost his trail when the copter had to set down.

Mary Miller still waited for some word of her daughter. With every day that passed, her hopes dimmed. If Kathy was still alive, Mary knew that she would come home on her birthday.

It is a Latvian superstition that when someone leaves a possession behind, the owner will one day return, and so Kathy's grandmother, Rosalie Purgalis, had continued to work on the dress that she was making for Kathy's birthday: May 23. Kathy would be sixteen on that day, a birthday she had looked forward to eagerly. She had been promised a ten-speed bike, and Mary had gone ahead and purchased it. If she didn't buy the bike, it would mean admitting that there was no one to give it to. . . .

Now detectives asked Mary if she would agree to meet with the media again, to ask the public if someone might come forward with new information. She agreed, and full-page stories appeared in all the Seattle newspapers on Kathy's birthday. There was Kathy's picture, a slightly blurred photo of a sweetly smiling girl with long hair. There were clear pictures of Mary Miller, the strain of the long wait showing on her face, and of Mark Walker—probably the last person to see Kathy alive beyond her abductor. And there was another blurred picture—a picture of Harvey taken by a surveillance camera, his face set in a frowning mask.

The gloves were off. Harvey had begun to detest Billy Baughman and Duane Homan, the two detectives who seemed to block his way wherever he turned. He refused to speak to the press about the case, saying his attorney had advised him not to. But he did charge that he, his family, and his associates were being harassed by the police.

"Those two—that Homan and Baughman—they're zeroing in on me because of my felony record."

And perhaps they were; the man had been convicted of attempted-rape/murder, assault to commit rape, and an assortment of burglaries. It would take a pair of fairly forgiving detectives to overlook that.

7

A normal man might have buckled under the stress of the investigation, but Harvey had never considered himself normal or average. He continued to work in his station, where business, surprisingly, was still brisk. His temper frayed easily, though, and he was annoyed by the interference of Alice's family, who had to go poking their noses into his business.

Alice had begged her brother not to confront Harvey, and she was frightened when she answered the door one night at ten and found her brother standing there.

"Don't say anything to Harvey," she begged.

Her brother didn't answer, but pushed his way into the house and sat down on the couch. Harvey walked out of the kitchen and seemed surprised, but he opened a beer for his brother-in-law.

The brother had more guts than sense and he looked at Harvey and said, "Have you been reading the papers—about that missing girl?"

Again Harvey looked startled, but he didn't respond.

"Just shut up," Alice pleaded.

"No . . . let him talk," Harvey said. "What else do you know about this?"

"It just seems strange that you were gone from the station that day for six hours." And now the brother inprovised, "And someone saw you pick her up."

Harvey said nothing.

"Why did you kill her?"

"Please, shut up!" Alice begged.

Harvey remained silent, but he stood up, and the brother tensed for a blow and took a crescent wrench out of his pocket.

And then the fight started. Not surprisingly, Harvey won with a blow to his brother-in-law's eye.

Alice's brother called the police and said he was worried about Alice. "I think she only stays because she's afraid of what Harvey might do to her. I think she's scared to death of him. Both the kids had to leave because of what he did to them, and I'm afraid for Alice."

Alice herself was beginning to wonder, although she subscribed absolutely to the premise that a wife always stands by her husband. She had already lost her children because of her devotion to Harvey. If she had to be estranged from the rest of her family too, she would—because everyone was picking on Harvey and he needed her. Yet there were questions that haunted her. Why had Harvey thrown away a perfectly good pair of new work boots? He'd worn them during the first week of May, and then he'd burned them, saying they weren't any good anymore. She'd seen them, and they looked in perfect condition to her.

Detectives Homan and Baughman received a call from a man who lived in Everett—with information that sounded as if it might have more meat to it than the previous calls in the growing log of citizen tips.

"I heard something next door to my house on that night—on the second of May. It was about five-thirty or six in the evening. There's nobody living in that place, but I heard a young girl scream two or three times, and then I heard someone moan. Later that night I heard a car out in the alley, and then a sound like a trunk slamming. This is a quiet neighborhood and we don't have much ruckus. I didn't connect the sounds with the girl that's missing until I read about her in the paper and about how her books were found out at the plywood place. As the crow flies, the plywood company is about two blocks away from here, and maybe two-tenths of a mile if you drive around."

Duane Homan and Detective Dick Reed went to the house in question, and found it securely locked. When they got inside, they found no evidence at all that anyone had been there. It appeared to have been deserted for many months. A thick mantle of dust lay over everything. Neither the windows nor the doors had been jimmied. Odd—but seemingly an unrelated incident.

Kathy was still missing.

Harvey continued to refuse to take a polygraph test.

The suspect had become surprisingly congenial now—apparently confident that there was no way the detectives could connect him to Kathy's disappearance. He suggested that perhaps they should be looking in other directions.

"Harvey," Homan said, "the sooner you come in to take the polygraph, the sooner we can allay Mrs. Miller's fears."

"I know she's worried. That's why I'm telling you you should be checking into other suspects."

"You're assuming you're the only one we're looking at, Harvey. That's not true. We just think you could clear a lot of things up if you'd sit still for the polygraph."

Harvey only smiled.

During the third week in May, Harvey and Alice agreed to come into the station to talk with Homan and Baughman. Harvey announced that he would not take the lie-detector test at all; his attorney had advised him against it.

"No way will I take that test."

Harvey sounded confident, but the detectives noted that he hadn't slept recently and that he had at least a day's growth of beard.

"I'm claiming police harassment and I'm going to keep telling the papers that," he threatened.

Baughman and Homan noticed that Harvey watched his wife carefully, as if he expected her to say something that might hurt his case. However, when the detectives asked to speak with Alice alone, Harvey opened his mouth to protest and then said nothing.

Alice told them that she and Harvey had made two trips to Canada since the girl had disappeared. She had stayed with him the whole time—in fact, he wanted her with him all the time.

"Nothing unusual happened on these trips?" Baughman asked.

She shook her head. "Oh, one thing. I found a button in the car when we were traveling. I asked Harvey where it had come from and he said it was probably Candy Erling's."

"Do you have it now?" The detectives were excited; this might be the first piece of physical evidence. "Where is it?"

"No, it's gone. Harvey said to give it to him and he would get rid of it."

"What did it look like?"

"Just a button. I don't think I'd recognize it if I saw it again."

"When did you see it?"

"I'm sure it was the weekend after the girl came up missing—that would have been . . . let me see, May fifth and sixth."

"Anything else that worries you?"

"Well, Harvey just won't let me out of his sight, ever since the girl disappeared. That's kind of strange, because he was never like that before. He always needed time alone before, but now we're together all the time."

Homam and Baughman could see that the strain was beginning to get to Alice Carignan. The devoted wife was betraying a certain lack of confidence in her husband. They were not surprised when, within a few days, Alice Carignan abandoned Harvey.

It was to be the beginning of her vacillation between utter terror of and repentant loyalty to her husband. Harvey had always affected the women in his life that way. When he had them, he considered them impediments to his womanizing. But when they left him, he was desolate. Alice belonged to him. It was that simple and he could not bear it when she rejected him. He was a master manipulator of females, possessed of charm that did not correlate with his hulking appearance and constant glower.

Alice contacted Billy Baughman and Duane Homan and told them she was in hiding, and her brother was helping her.

She was afraid to stay more than a night or two in one spot for fear Harvey would track her down.

Harvey had a great many problems now: stakeout crews were watching him around the clock, his wife was hiding from him, and it was difficult to keep his mind on business. When he went to his mother-in-law's house to find out where Alice was, he found the house empty. His mother-in-law was hiding too.

Alice was afraid to return to her house to get her clothing and the other necessities she'd left behind. She asked Homan and Baughman to accompany her. They did so, and she showed them the vacuum bag—which still contained the dust from the suspect Toronado. "I vacuumed Harvey's Oldsmobile out with that, and the stuff is still in the bag. I guess you can take it if you want."

They took the dust bag and the attachment brush she'd used to clean out the purple car. They already had gleaned some of Kathy Miller's hair from a hairbrush left behind. With any luck, criminalists in the lab working with a scanning electron microscope might find hairs in the dust bag that matched Kathy Miller's hair in class and characteristics.

But they had no luck at all. This case had been saturated with bad luck from the beginning. The analysts in the crime lab found nothing in the bag which might be connected to Kathy.

It was extremely difficult for Billy Baughman and Duane Homan to explain to Mary Miller why they could not go into Harvey's property with a search warrant at the very least, and why they could not arrest him at the very most. Their hands were still tied by legal restrictions.

Mary had come to a kind of resignation; she knew that Kathy was dead now. Her birthday had come and gone, and Kathy had not come home. The ten-speed bicycle that Kathy had yearned for remained in its box.

Alice Carignan was constantly on the move, and getting more jittery every time she called in to Homicide. She wondered if she might safely stay at her mother's home, and the detectives could only tell her to use her own best judgment. They doubted that Harvey would hurt her, if only because he was trying to continue his charade as an innocent man hounded by police. Killing his wife would put him on a one-way path back to the penitentiary in Walla Walla.

The word was out that Harvey, in fact, was getting ready to split; his fondness for the Northwest had diminished. Informants called to say that he was clearing up his affairs in the Seattle area, saying good-bye to acquaintances, and talking of moving back to Minnesota.

There was nothing Billy Baughman and Duane Homan could do to stop him. He was still as free to come and go as any man on the street. It galled them, but there it was.

Mary Miller received a phone call that shocked her. Georgia Johnson, Alice's daughter, called to convey her sympathy and to relate the way that Harvey had frightened her when she'd lived at home. It was not a comforting phone call, but Mary had already faced the possibility that her daughter was dead, that she had been seized by a sex pervert. She thanked Georgia for her concern, wondering what kind of life Harvey's stepdaughter must have had.

Mary had another visit from someone close to the case—or from someone she suspected was very close to the case. She was called from her desk at the bank and told someone wanted to see her. When she went to the counter, she saw a woman in her sixties—a woman who refused to identify herself.

The woman stared at Mary for a long time, and then she said, "You've got the wrong man. . . ."

Mary could only assume that the woman was Harvey's mother, but when she tried to question the older woman, she walked swiftly out of the bank.

On May 29 Homan and Baughman came, almost unerringly, so close to where Kathy waited for discovery. With all of the state of Washington and the vast stretches of wilderness beyond the Canadian border, it seems uncanny that they should have decided to drive to the Tulalip Indian Reservation north of Everett to conduct an interview in their search for the girl missing now for four weeks. They had talked to everyone who knew Harvey Carignan, everyone except a woman he had been known to visit in the past: Kathy Sylvester.

Mrs. Sylvester lived in a sparsely populated area on the edge of acres and acres of wilderness area on the Indian reservation. She told them that she had not seen Harvey for some time but that he had called her the week before.

"He was looking for his wife, and I told him I hadn't seen her."

"Has he been up here on the reservation recently?"

"Not as far as I know."

The detective pair looked out over the woods and vegetation on the reservation and felt a chill. A man could bury a body here and be confident that it would never be found.

Homan and Baughman had checked everywhere for Harvey's first wife, Sheila, but she seemed to have disappeared from the face of the earth. When they received a bulletin from the Royal Canadian Mounted Police regarding the unidentified body of a woman found in British Columbia, a body wrapped in a faded blanket, they wondered. Canada was one of Harvey's favorite stamping grounds, and the general description of the woman matched the first Mrs. Carignan in age and size.

A check of Harvey's traffic-violation record also startled them. The Seattle detectives knew that the Island County Sheriff's Office was still working on the unsolved homicide of a young woman who had vanished on October 15, 1972. One of Harvey Carignan's traffic tickets had been written in Mount Vernon, Washington, on October 15, 1972. Mount Vernon was a direct route to Whidbey Island, and just south of Bellingham where the victim—Laura Leslie Brock—had lived.

They called Undersheriff Bob Sharp of Island County, and he agreed that Harvey Carignan's presence along the route where Laura Brock was last seen hitchhiking might be more than coincidence.

In one of the bleak ironies of the Kathy Miller case, *this* girl—nineteen-year-old Laura Brock—was the girl that Mary had read the newspaper articles about, the murder victim whose story Kathy had heard, prompting her promise that she would never hitchhike.

"What are the details on your case?" Homan asked Sharp.

"Our girl was seen when she was picked up," Sharp said.

"She got into a pickup truck with a silver canopy. It had some kind of a pipe sticking out horizontally near the gas tank. The driver appeared to the witnesses to be a middle-aged white male."

"Anything else?" Homan asked. "A partial license number even?"

"Nobody saw the driver closely, and nobody got a license number. We found the body sometime later just off an old logging road in a very isolated spot up here on Whidbey. She was naked except for knee-high stockings. The cause of death was bludgeoning to the head. The whole left side of her head was crushed. She fought. She had a few strands of gray-brown hair in one hand. Our lab people think it's from the chest of the man who killed her."

It seemed too close to be a coincidence. But Laura Brock's murder had been accomplished by someone clever enough not to leave strong clues. The Whidbey Island detectives still considered it an open case, and leads had dwindled in the six months since the pretty coed's body had been discovered.

Alice Carignan called Homan and Baughman again. She had decided to get an annulment. She now believed that her husband had killed Kathy Miller.

"I left a note for him on the refrigerator, asking him to tell me the truth. I told him that if he would just tell the truth, then maybe we could get back together. He called me and said that that was a big responsibility.

"He wants me to meet him one more time and talk things over. He said he'd meet me at Sambo's and tell me everything."

It looked good. At last there seemed to be a chance for a break in the case, although the detectives couldn't imagine that Alice, in her naiveté, could convince Harvey to confess. Sending Alice to break Harvey was a little like sending a bunny rabbit to reason with Attila the Hun.

Still, Homan and Baughman staked out Sambo's. They saw Harvey Carignan drive up and go into the restaurant. Alice was not there. Harvey left, but he returned three or four times to scan the busy restaurant. Finally he drove away and didn't come back.

Alice called the detectives later. "I couldn't go. I was afraid of him."

It was June now. The cherry and apple blossoms had faded and fallen away from the trees, and roses bloomed all over Seattle. The weather was hot, and vegetation grew thicker and thicker, hiding secrets still undiscovered.

Kathy was still missing.

8

From the moment she realized that Kathy had vanished, Mary Miller had been consumed with a terrible need for haste. It had seemed that if only everyone would mobilize to look for her daughter, Kathy could still be found and rescued. At first Mary and her family appeared to be the only ones who were passionately concerned about Kathy's disappearance—their whole lives taken up with finding her. Slowly Mary had come to trust Duane Homan and Billy Baughman. She sensed that the search was as important to them as if it were one of *their* daughters who was lost. She had come to dread weekends and holidays, fearful that the search would be temporarily abandoned, but then she saw that Homan and Baughman kept right on working regardless of the day. Mary talked to them by phone each day, sometimes several times a day.

One thought burned inside Mary: Harvey Carignan knew what had happened to Kathy. He had admitted coming to Sears where Kathy had waited, but Mary was sure he lied when he said he had never seen her. His refusal to take a lie-detector test only clinched her suspicions about him.

"Why can't you just go in and search his house . . . and his garage, and his cars?" she asked the detectives for what seemed like the hundredth time.

"The prosecutor says we don't have enough probable cause," Baughman explained patiently. "We have no physical evidence and we don't even have one witness who actually *saw* him with Kathy."

"Then shake it out of him," Mary cried. "Force him to talk!"

"We can't do that," Billy Baughman answered. "In the old days . . . well, things were different then. Not now. He has his constitutional rights. We can't violate them, or anything we got out of him would be excluded. We couldn't use it in court anyway."

"What about *Kathy's* constitutional rights?" Mary asked.

Duane Homan looked at the floor and then said painfully, "Under our present system, I'm afraid the victim doesn't have the constitutional rights that the suspect has."

This seemed incomprehensible to Mary, and yet, when she called the prosecutor's office herself, she was given essentially the same information. Victims' rights were nowhere near as clearly defined as those of suspects. Since no one knew what had happened to Kathy—whether she was alive or dead—Kathy had no rights.

Another weekend came. It was Saturday, June 2, one month to the day since Kathy had walked away into a kind of endless twilight. Strangely, Mary had begun to feel a lessening of tension; if not peace, the beginning of acceptance. She knew that Kathy was never coming home. Perhaps it was the fact that it had been exactly a month since Kathy had vanished; perhaps it was something more ephemeral.

Mary talked that morning with Baughman and Homan, and they too could sense a calmness, the dull acknowledgment of what must be.

The next day they found Kathy.

On that Sunday morning, two sixteen-year-old boys were riding their motorbikes along the narrow roads that crisscross the Tulalip Indian Reservation north of Everett. They stopped to pick salmonberries growing in the brush just off the Water Works Road, and were pushing their way into the dense vegetation just before noon when they suddenly caught a trace of alien odor on the wind. It was the sickly-sweet smell of death.

One of the boys walked farther into the brush and saw a figure there, something or someone wrapped in a shroud of black plastic sheeting. The youth shouted to his friend, "Come back in here. See if it looks to you like it looks to me!"

It did. The wrapped figure seemed surely to be a body, and the boys did not attempt to investigate further. They rode on their motorbikes to the Tulalip Tribal Office two miles away. There they called the Snohomish County Sheriff's Office and were instructed to return to the intersection of the Tulalip Road and Water Works Road to await the arrival of deputies and lead them in.

Deputy K. Engelbretson in Unit 36 arrived at the site at one-fifteen P.M., followed within minutes by Patrol Sergeant Alan Halliday. The deputies recognized the witnesses; John Bingham, sixteen, was a nephew of the chief of police of the hamlet of Arlington, Washington.

Halliday and Engelbretson walked into the woods about fifteen feet and saw a log that blocked the narrow, rough trail. Beyond the log the officers could see the outlines of a human form beneath the black plastic. On closer perusal they could see that the body was nude. It had lain in this sylvan bower for a long time, so long that the deputies could not determine if the corpse was that of a male or female or how death might have occurred.

Halliday activated his portable radio and called for assistance from Detective Sergeant Tom Hart and the coroner's office.

None of the investigators from Snohomish County realized yet the magnitude of the discovery. They had no idea whose body they had found. The victim might well have been left there after a family dispute had exploded into violence, or after some drunken melee in a tavern. Identification would have to wait. Whatever had happened to the victim had happened a long time before—possibly months before. There was no need to hurry now. The important thing was to be sure the scene was thoroughly searched for any clues that might have been left behind by the killer or killers.

The scene itself was deceptively peaceful as the officers talked in hushed tones; daisies dotted the bright green grass, and wild roses grew in tangled clusters. The only sounds beyond their own voices came from birds and the whisper of wind through the trees. The figure of the victim lay on its side, one hand tucked beneath the chin as if he or she had only lain down in the woods for a nap.

Detective Hart went over the area with a metal detector in an effort to locate a possible murder weapon or some other small clues that might lie hidden beneath the undergrowth. He came up with a few beer-bottle caps, long rusted, but nothing of value.

Beyond the body site there was a kind of bootleg dump where old car parts and debris had been thrown away. And the region had obviously been used as a lovers' lane. It was isolated enough to attract those who wanted privacy—more than a quarter of a mile from the nearest home.

Coroner Lorri Hudson examined the body at the scene and determined that death had undoubtedly occurred at least a month before. There were two nickel-sized holes apparent in the right rear of the skull. Moreover, there was a large area of crushing to the skull on the left side just behind the ear, evidence of trauma from a heavy weapon.

The victim had excellent teeth, and they had been carefully cared for with dental work. The hair was light brown or blond, and longish, but in the era of long-haired males, this would not be positive proof of sex. The fingernails were small and well-kept, possibly those of a woman who cared for her appearance.

"It didn't happen here," Hart said. "There are no clothes here at all. I think the murder took place somewhere else, and then the victim was wrapped in plastic and brought here."

Soil and vegetation samples were taken and bagged for the crime lab. The victim's hands too were encased in plastic, secured with rubber bands at the wrist, to protect the fingertips for possible print identification.

At three P.M. the body was removed and taken to Everett to await autopsy.

The Snohomish County detectives cleared the body site then and fanned out along the Water Works Road to canvass nearby residents.

The woman who lived in the nearest house said that she had not seen or heard anything unusual for weeks. She thought the woods property belonged to a man who lived in a trailer at the far end of the Water Works Road. But when the man himself was contacted, he said he had no idea how the body had come to be on his acreage.

A check of missing persons reported in Snohomish County netted no possibles. Sergeant Hart stopped by the Everett Police Department and obtained their list of currently missing persons. They had no one who might have matched the victim found on the reservation.

And then he called the Seattle Police Department. When he described the victim as having been five feet, seven or eight with blond hair, his call was transferred at once to Duane Homan and Billy Baughman.

The detective team had expected that the call would come one day, and still it was a shock. Harvey Carignan had been followed over the mountains, to the Canadian border, all over the Seattle area, and now it seemed that Kathy's body had been left on the Tulalip Reservation—such a short distance from where they had questioned Harvey's friend Mrs. Sylvester. In a way, it figured: the Indian reservation was not very far from the plywood firm where Kathy's books had been left.

But when they had questioned Kathy Sylvester, they had been convinced that she knew nothing about Kathy Miller. The woman had appeared only to be a platonic friend of Harvey's, an older woman, and surprised and concerned when they'd approached her.

Before they called Mary Miller, they wanted to be sure. They did not want to put her through the agony of thinking that this body was her daughter's—not until they were positive that it was.

Homan and Baughman had Kathy's dental charts. Mary had seen that both of her children always had dental care; now these charts might serve a more tragic purpose.

On June 4 Pathologist Dr. Emanuel Bitar tentatively identified the body found on the Tulalip property as Kathy Miller after comparing the victim's teeth with the dental chart.

"First permanent molars—right and left—silver fillings on biting surfaces. In addition, one small silver filling on left first permanent molar . . . outside surface. This outside filling is indicated on dental chart of Katherine Sue Miller. . . ."

An unusual filling, this last entry, and almost absolute proof that it was indeed Kathy who had lain so long in the lonely woods. And all of the searching would not have saved her.

At eight A.M. that Monday, the autopsy began with Homan and Baughman in attendance along with the Snohomish County detectives.

Kathy had sustained tremendous blows to the head from a heavy blunt instrument. The cheekbone—the lateral orbit of the left eye—was fractured. There were smaller areas of damage on the right side—the "nickel-sized holes" seen by Coroner Hudson.

"What weapon?" Baughman asked quietly.

"This would be consistent with a two-by-four," Bitar replied, "or a hammer—possibly a tire iron. There are at least three blows, maybe four. A blunt instrument swung repeatedly."

And then some small comfort for those who had loved Kathy. She would have been unconscious with the first blow, and dead within moments. She would not have had time to be frightened or to feel pain. . . .

The perpetrator of such a crime? Homan and Baughman pondered that, and they each visualized an immensely strong man in the grip of a homicidal rage.

Neither would allow himself to think of the pictures of the shyly smiling young girl who had been Kathy Miller.

They would have to tell Mary Miller now that Kathy was dead, and they dreaded it as much as anything they had ever had to do. Perhaps delaying—as they wished they could do forever—the two detectives drove to the body site on the Tulalip Reservation before they returned to Seattle. They could see where a vehicle had been parked with its motor running; the grass and soil still bore the discoloration from exhaust burns. The driver had not tarried long, only stopped his vehicle long enough to rid it of its incriminating burden.

Whoever had left Kathy here, he had been shrewd, fully aware of the dangerousness of physical evidence. The body had been carefully swaddled in the black Visqueen so that no blood would mark the killer's vehicle, and the victim's clothing had been thrown away someplace else. Kathy's books had been dumped a few miles away in the plywood firm's parking lot. No, the murderer had not intended to leave even minuscule signs that might led back to him.

Duane Homan and Billy Baughman drove to the Purgalis's house, where Mary Miller waited for them. The discovery of the unidentified body had somehow been leaked to the media, and Mary had heard it. She let the detectives in and offered them a seat without asking why they had come. She knew why, and she could not change it. But she needed time, some way to delay what they would tell her.

"Mrs. Miller," Duane Homan began. "Mary . . . the dental charts from your dentist . . . there was a perfect match with a body found north of Everett. We've been up there today. Mary, it was Kathy."

"You're sure? You're absolutely sure?"

"Yes. . . ."

Mary's eyes brimmed with tears, but she did not cry. She stared back at them quite calmly, trying to find words. It was typical of Mary Miller that even as she dealt with the news, she was concerned about the detectives' feelings.

"I've conditioned myself to this for the last thirty days, but it doesn't make it any easier. Thank you for finding my daughter."

"The case isn't finished," Billy Baughman said. "We'll continue to work on it until we find a way . . . as long as it takes. As long as we're policemen."

As he spoke, none of them could know just how long it was going to take, or how much horror still lay ahead.

9

To the layman, it would seem that now murder charges would certainly be filed against Harvey Carignan. The body of the victim had been found. Kathy Miller was no longer only a missing person. Kathy was dead, murdered by someone who had taken her from a busy commercial intersection to some killing place, and then to the lonely isolation of the Tulalip Reservation.

Homan and Baughman drove from the corner in front of the Sears store to the body site, and noted that it was forty-two miles one way. The round-trip driving time would have taken seventy to eighty minutes. The trail where the body was left was 1.2 miles from the home of Carignan's friend Kathy Sylvester. Harvey himself was reported to have once owned property on the Tulalip Reservation, and often drove there to visit Mrs. Sylvester.

Yes, it would seem that murder charges were imminent—but the legal processes were hampered by the complete lack of physical evidence, and now Duane Homan and Billy Baughman increased the pace of their investigation. They were concerned that Harvey Carignan might bolt and run at any time and leave their jurisdiction, that he might even leave the country. He had little to keep him in the Seattle area, and much to avoid.

His employees at the Sav-Mor noticed that Harvey was getting antsy. He pulled at his face constantly, and so ferociously it looked as if he was trying to pull it off. His twitching was as bad as they'd ever seen it, and he perspired so much that he was forever wiping his forehead with his handkerchief. Everything seemed to irritate Harvey, and he actually frightened the men who worked for him when his temper exploded.

One of Harvey's employees warned Homan, "You've never seen anyone get mad the way Harvey does. I've seen him so angry that he picked the whole front end of his truck off the ground and slammed it down. If you're going to take him, you'd better get the first blow in—or it will be rough to subdue him. Don't ever let him get a hold of you; he won't let up until he crushes you."

Alice Carignan had left Harvey, apparently for good, and he seemed to have little enthusiasm for his business. Harvey did have family in the area—his mother and stepfather, who lived in West Seattle—but he had family in the Minneapolis area too, and the detective team assumed that Minnesota must beckon to their suspect seductively.

And yet Harvey was tenacious when it came to clinging to the women who "belonged" to him. He seemed compelled to badger them until they returned to him. Wherever Sheila Carignan was, his first wife had apparently found it necessary to go underground to avoid him. Alice Carignan was still moving from place to place so that she would not have to confront him.

Harvey, as anxious as he was to get out of town, would not leave until he talked to Alice. He had always been able to convince Alice that the sky was green if he wanted to, and he still thought he could.

He spent a lot of time thinking about his situation. Certain things had not gone as he'd planned them. The friends who he'd been sure would alibi for him had reneged, Candy Erling had apparently spilled her stupid little guts to the police— painting him as a seducer of young girls—and Alice had asked too many questions when he'd decided to throw away his boots, nagging at him and reminding him he'd had the boots for only three months. His brother-in-law had had to stick his nose into things too. They were all breathing down his neck and getting in his way. But the worst of all were the cops. He hated Duane Homan and Billy Baughman most of all. They seemed always to be sneaking around, checking on him, asking questions. He made it a point of looking over his shoulder now wherever he went to see who was following him. He wasn't sure if the cars behind him were police sneakers, but he heard the rotors of the pigs' helicopter overhead. There was no question about it: his constitutional rights were being violated and somebody was going to pay for that. He'd studied enough when he was inside the joint, and he knew the law and he knew that they didn't have anything on him. Nothing.

At this point Duane Homan and Billy Baughman would have had to agree with Harvey. They didn't have anything concrete. The one piece of physical evidence was the black plastic that had been found with the body. Visqueen. A common product used by builders to keep house foundations dry, used by landscapers to keep weeds from growing under Beauty Bark. And used by Harvey Carignan to wrap gasoline pumps that were not currently in service. They managed to find a sample of the black plastic used on the Sav-Mor pumps. A partial roll of it still rested in the attic of the garage of the home Harvey had shared with Alice. But technicians at the police crime lab found that it was not from the same lot as the Visqueen wrapped around Kathy Miller's body. They had been sure that it would match, and the news from the lab was a bitter disappointment, just as the analysis of the contents of the vacuum-cleaner bag had been.

There still was no physical evidence. The button Alice had found the weekend after Kathy disappeared was lost forever, and none of Kathy's clothing had been found despite a concentrated search of the Tulalip Reservation. The clothes that Harvey had worn on May 2 and 3 had been washed many times and would be useless for examination for bloodstains.

There were the schoolbooks found at the plywood mill. If only . . . if only Harvey's prints, or even a small section of a print that tied in with his, could be found on the pages of those abandoned books. That would be enough to show that he had been with Kathy. But the timekeeper had wiped those books off because they were wet with rain.

I.D. technician Karl C. Jepsen worked for days over the algebra book. Using the ninhydrin process, he was able to isolate portions of two fingerprints from a sheet of notebook paper tucked between the textbook's pages, an assignment dated April 30, 1973, and marked "A+, B+." The prints had come from the left index and left middle finger of the person who had touched that page. However, when Jepsen compared the prints to those on file for Harvey Carignan, they hadn't matched.

The ninhydrin process for developing latent prints on paper is a miraculous thing; prints left a half-century earlier can be lifted from paper with this procedure. But the prints on Kathy's assignment seemed worthless for evidentiary use.

Now that Kathy's body had been found, Jepsen worked to obtain her fingerprints. The fact that most teenagers have never been fingerprinted is often a roadblock in police investigations. They have never been in the armed services, have never applied for jobs that require security clearance and fingerprinting, so when young bodies are found, there may not be a positive way to identify them.

Because Kathy's body had lain exposed to the elements for a month, her fingertips were dried and shriveled from the sun and would not give good prints. Jepsen soaked her hands and fingers in a three-percent solution of sodium hydroxide to soften them and then applied a three-percent solution of formaldehyde until the top layer sloughed off and the ridges beneath appeared. Photographs and impressions were taken and Jepsen was finally able to isolate a usable set of prints.

Comparing these prints to the algebra paper, he found what he had expected: the prints on the school papers were Kathy's.

It seemed as if the fates themselves were conspiring with the suspect to hide all traces of evidence that might connect him solidly with the murder of Kathy Miller.

There were witnesses to somewhat suspicious behavior on Harvey's part, and now some of them came forward tentatively to report their feelings. Rod Sloane had reported the alibi attempt, the transparent lie about the ex-cons that Harvey "had had to kill," and now another man recalled being in the Carignan home a week or so after Kathy vanished.

"I said to Harvey and Alice that the girl was probably a runaway and would turn up anytime," and Harvey, he says, 'I'll kiss your ass if she turns up alive. . . .'"

On June 14 a call came into headquarters that looked like the break that Homan and Baughman had sought for so long. A man called and said, "I gave Harvey Carignan some black Visqueen. I have the other end of the roll."

The detective answering the phone asked for the man's name, but he refused to identify himself. He did, however, promise to call at three-forty-five when Homan and Baughman came on duty to work the night shift.

The informant did call back, and he turned over the remainder of the roll of black plastic. In the laboratory, the detectives held their breaths as the fresh roll was placed next to the Visqueen taken from the body and the edges approximated.

The tears did not match.

"He must have torn it again before he used it," Baughman said bitterly. "Where's the piece that matches?"

"Gone," said Homan. "Gone, like everything else."

They had yet to get a go-ahead on a search warrant for Harvey's purple Toronado, although they doubted that it would be of much help now to process that car. Harvey had had six weeks to wash and vacuum it.

"We're going to lose him," Homan said flatly. "He's going to get in that car one of these days soon and he'll be gone, and there's not a damn thing we can do to stop him. We don't even have a traffic warrant on him. Right now, today, we'd be lucky to arrest him for jaywalking."

"He knocked Alice around. She could charge him with assault."

"She won't. She's afraid of him one minute, and the next minute she's thinking about reconciling with him. Either way, I don't think that she's liable to file assault charges against him."

Harvey Carignan's customers were dwindling. His picture had appeared in the papers under headlines about Kathy Miller's murder. An employee called Homan and Baughman and reported that a customer had asked Harvey point-blank if he'd killed Kathy.

"Harvey started sweating and pulling on his face like he does, and he told the guy not to say such things. I thought you guys were picking on him, but now I'm beginning to worry about my own daughters. Harvey gets turned on by fourteen- to eighteen-year-old girls, and he doesn't care how crude he is when he talks to them or who's around when he says it. And I might as well tell you, Harvey's really saying good-bye to people now. He's heading out."

"When?" Baughman asked.

"I'm not sure." There was a long silence on the line. "There's something else I'd better tell you—for your own protection. Harvey showed me this hammer—this new ball-peen hammer. He holds it out, and he smiles, and he says . . . he says . . ."

"What did he say?"

"He says, 'This is to take care of Homan and Baughman.' He wants to crush your heads before he leaves."

Billy Baughman and Duane Homan took the threat seriously. They had little doubt that Harvey would relish killing them. Nevertheless, they were determined to search his vehicles before he left Seattle.

At long last, the detective team's pleas to the prosecutor that a search warrant for the Toronado was essential were successful. One loophole in the Fourth Amendment which protects the citizen from unreasonable searches and seizures can be utilized when the item to be searched is a vehicle. Because a vehicle can "be quickly moved out of the locality or jurisdiction in which the warrant is sought," cars known to be on their way out of state can be searched. While Homan and Baughman waited for word that the search warrant had been signed by a judge, members of the Tact Squad observed Harvey in front of his mother's home in West Seattle on June 19 at six-thirty-five in the evening. He was moving some of his possessions into his mother's house, apparently storing his things there in preparation for a trip. If the warrant did not arrive before Harvey left, they would be helpless to stop him.

Harvey emptied the truck and drove off.

Shortly before seven, the warrant, signed by Judge Quigley, was delivered to Homan and Baughman, and they sped toward West Seattle. At their hand signal, a tow truck backed into place in front of the purple Toronado, parked there and hooked onto its bumper.

At that moment Harvey drove up. He saw the tow truck, and he bailed out of his pickup and walked furiously up to the Oldsmobile. Then he spotted Duane Homan standing there. Homan had never seen the suspect so angry. Harvey reached back into the truck. Homan expected to see the new ball-peen hammer in his hand.

Billy Baughman unloosed his service revolver from his holster, prepared to protect his partner.

Harvey spotted Baughman, and brought his hands out—empty. But he was still mad as hell.

"What's going on here? What do you think you're doing?" Harvey pulled at his face unconsciously as he protested.

"We have a search warrant for your Toronado," Homan replied. "Would you like to read it?"

Harvey glanced at it with a half-smile, half-sneer, and the tension of the moment passed. "You could have searched my car anytime. I don't need to see a warrant."

"Are you planning to leave Seattle, Harvey?" Homan asked.

"I'm going to Denver to look for a job."

"How long do you think you'll be gone?"

"Six to eight days."

The tow truck began to pull its burden away from the curb, and Homan turned to Harvey. "We'll be seeing you."

Harvey Carignan stared back at the men who had dogged his trail, and attempted a look of bravado.

But he couldn't manage it; the beads of sweat broke free from his forehead and coursed down his face.

In the Seattle police garage, the Toronado awaited the ministrations of Jean Battista and Don MacLaren, crime-lab criminalists. It was photographed, vacuumed, and any latent prints were lifted from it. It was dirty and full of junk: an empty pint of whiskey under the backseat, a scattering (for some reason) of plastic baby's blocks, hamburger wrappings, an amphetamine pill, a few seeds that appeared to be marijuana. But there were no long blond hairs, no buttons, no torn scraps of blue-and-white fabric, no schoolbooks or papers. Nothing of Kathy Miller.

Jean Battista found that all the windows had been wiped down inside and out. Almost all. The outside of the passenger window had been wiped clean, but not the inside. From that surface Ms. Battista lifted a print—a partial palm print.

It could have been the missing link, the one vital shred of evidence that would have stopped Harvey Carignan. The print was compared to Harvey Carignan's palm prints, and to Alice Carignan's palm prints, and it matched neither. It had come from a smallish hand, a woman's hand certainly. But, tragically, I.D. technician Jepsen had been unable to retrieve Kathy Miller's palm print. Only her fingerprints, and there were no fingerprints on the window that Harvey had overlooked. Only the palm print.

No one would ever be able to say absolutely that it was Kathy Miller's hand that had pressed against that window, perhaps in a vain attempt to escape.

There has never been a doubt in Duane Homan's or Billy Baughman's mind that that partial palm print on the passenger window of Harvey Carignan's purple Toronado was left by Kathy Sue Miller. Had her bludgeoned body been found soon enough, they could have had a print to compare. Fate and time had robbed the investigators of that vital clue, but the discovery indicated to them that Harvey was far from infallible. He thought he had erased all evidence from the Oldsmobile. Indeed, he had been nervous as he watched the car being towed away for processing, perhaps apprehensive that there still might be something left in the Toronado that could harm him. The overlooked palm print showed that Harvey had been a little careless. If he had made one mistake, he would make another—and another.

It was only a matter of time.

But the passage of time alarmed the two detectives. They were convinced that Harvey had killed not only Kathy Miller but also Laura Leslie Brock. Perhaps there were other bodies lying undiscovered in desolate areas. The manner of murder and the randomness of it could bode nothing but tragedy ahead; the roving, random killer never stops until he is apprehended. Their own powerlessness to stop him galled them. Harvey had hit the road again, driving his silver-canopied pickup truck and abandoning his suspect Oldsmobile.

The two detectives dreaded the possibility of future victims. They did not drop the probe simply because they suspected Harvey had run back to Minnesota, back to his old stomping grounds. They knew that he was obsessed with Alice and that he would be unable to stay away from her for very long. She had rejected him, and Harvey wouldn't allow that to continue.

He would be back.

Homan and Baughman talked with Harvey's mother and stepfather. They found his parents very protective of the son who had given them nothing but trouble from the time he was a child. His mother was reluctant to say anything that might connect her son to Kathy's murder, but the detectives could see the indecision in her eyes. She was not as positive of Harvey's innocence as she proclaimed.

"I'll have to agree," she said painfully, "that Harvey isn't telling the complete truth."

She tensed as they spelled out the circumstantial evidence linking Harvey to the brutal murder of a fifteen-year-old schoolgirl, and she seemed relieved when they switched the line of questioning to the whereabouts of Harvey's first wife, Sheila.

Sheila had vanished so completely that the detectives had begun to wonder if she might be the corpse discovered in British Columbia. Canadian Sergeant U. K. Bodner had shown great interest when Homan and Baughman laid out their case to him. So much interest, in fact, that he had made a trip to Seattle to compare notes with them.

"Our body was that of a woman believed to be in her mid-thirties to early forties—about the age of Sheila Carignan. We don't have the whole body—only the torso. She was wrapped in this blanket." He held up a Polaroid picture of a weathered, stained blanket with an unusual pattern.

"We can't even be sure of the cause of death, but somebody dumped that torso in the ditch. Our feeling is that the victim may have been brought up from the States. We've publicized the body discovery all over Canada, and no one's come forth with a positive identification. Not even close. All we really know is that she was Caucasian, medium weight, medium height, and that she'd borne at least one child."

"She was found in May of this year—1973. Right?" Baughman asked.

Bodner nodded. "But our pathologist estimates that she'd been dead since November last year."

"That would fit," Homan said. "Harvey made trips up to British Columbia often. His wife—his current wife—went with him usually, but she says he often left her alone for hours at a time, and she doesn't know where he went. He has an uncle up there that they've visited."

But now, as Bodner joined the Seattle detectives in questioning Harvey's mother, she shook her head. "Sheila's all right—at least she was the last I heard. I think I have her last address."

She looked through an address book and nodded. "Here. She's married again. Her name's Cooper or Hooper or something like that now."

After working through a series of forwarding addresses, the investigators found Sheila Carignan Cooper, alive and well—but very nervous. She was working as a part-time grocery clerk, and she begged the detectives not to reveal where she worked or where she lived. "I can't talk to you."

"You might have something to tell us that could be very important," Baughman urged.

"Let me think about it. I'll call you."

Sheila Carignan did eventually talk to Homan and Baughman.

"Tell us what you can about Harvey Carignan."

"I married him in 1969, and I divorced him in 1971. We were only married a short time when he was picked up for burglary and for carrying a gun. They dropped the burglary charges later, but they sent him back to prison for violating his parole."

Sheila voiced her fear of her ex-husband. "At the end of

our marriage, I knew he was about to do something to me—hurt me. He had a temper that you couldn't believe. I know I escaped because I managed to keep calm and I talked to him quietly. But the thing about Harvey is—he hates women. He hates women with a passion.''

The room was quiet. As the detectives stood to leave, Sheila looked up and asked, "Can you tell me something about the little girl—the Miller girl? How was she killed?''

The detectives explained the case to Harvey's first wife, and she nodded. ''You know, I have no doubt at all that he killed her. He's a very, very intelligent man. He keeps exact records about everything he does, either written or in his head. He's very methodical, but his temper . . . his rage . . .''

She shuddered, remembering.

Assured that her ex-husband was presently missing from the Seattle area, she seemed relieved.

Alice Carignan, however, remained ambivalent. She had moved back into her house, and started divorce proceedings, but somehow Harvey's bad points had begun to fade now that he was so far away. He wrote to her often, almost every day, and his letters were so full of love and tenderness. She was not ready to take him back, but she couldn't really tell him there wasn't any hope, either, not when she read the pages and pages of love thoughts he poured out to her. She did let Homan and Baughman know that Harvey was in Minneapolis, living with relatives, but more than that notification she was not prepared to give.

Duane Homan and Billy Baughman had no ambivalence at all. They prepared a dossier on Harvey Carignan, summaries of the murders of Laura Brock and Kathy Miller, and sent it to the Minneapolis Police Department, warning Minnesota police that Harvey was now in their bailiwick. The information was noted and filed away. At the moment, the Minnesota authorities had no cases whose M.O. resembled the crimes Harvey was suspected of on the West Coast. The Minnesota police couldn't follow Harvey around waiting for him to do something.

After a while, nobody remembered the packet of information sent from Seattle—not even the clerk who'd filed it away.

Although Harvey Carignan was now living more than two thousand miles away, Duane Homan and Billy Baughman did not forget about him. The thick case files that held all the paperwork on Kathy Miller's murder still rested on their desks, and the two men looked through them often, seeking the one route that they might not yet have explored.

II

Minnesota

10

Harvey Carignan had told Detectives Homan and Baughman that he was heading for Colorado the last time they'd seen him. Whether he intended to go to Denver at that time, or whether he was merely trying to throw them off his trail is not known. What is known is that he did not turn his pickup truck to the east. Instead, he headed south into California. He undoubtedly drove all night on June 19, 1973, because the next day found him in Solano County.

Harvey was cited for speeding in that California county on June 20. Although he delighted in using the freeways here and then there and then someplace else as a means of being hundreds of miles away, he invariably left a trail with his traffic tickets.

The California ticket would one day be of great interest to Detective Sergeant Erwin Carlstedt of Sonoma County. Carlstedt was dealing with a rash of murders of young women in his jurisdiction in the early seventies. Between February 1972 and December 1973, six women were found murdered in the Santa Rosa area of Sonoma County—which adjoins Solano County, where Harvey was pulled over for speeding.

All of the young women were nude, and no clothing or personal possessions were found near their bodies. Further, between May and July of 1973, four more naked female bodies were found in San Francisco, south of the Sonoma-Solano area. Still another young woman's corpse was found off Interstate 5 near Redding, California, in July 1973.

Even today, ten years later, there is no way to tie Harvey in with any of those killings. In common with the victims attributed to Harvey, none of them had been strangled. One had succumbed to a tremendous blow to the back of the head, and seven of the eleven had been raped. Of the eleven, one was totally out of the pattern suspected in Harvey's M.O.; she had been poisoned.

Whatever his activities may have been in northern California, Harvey did not stay in that state long. He soon had traveled cross-country to his former home, Minnesota, and a half-brother living in Minneapolis took him into his home.

On June 28 a Minneapolis woman, Marlys Townsend, waited for a bus on a deserted street corner. Suddenly there was someone behind her, the sound of the scrape of a boot or shoe sliding across the sidewalk, heavy breathing. But before she could turn around, something slammed into the back of her head and she fell, unconscious.

When she came to, she found that she was in a pickup truck, a truck driven by a huge balding man. Still foggy and in pain, she was horrified when the man grabbed her hand and attempted to place it on his genitals.

"Touch me," he barked.

She pulled away and grabbed frantically for the door handle next to her. The man saw what she was doing and swore at her, seizing her hair in his hand to stop her from tumbling out.

What he did not know was that she was wearing a wig. She pulled free of his grasp, leaving her wig behind, still clenched in her startled attacker's hand. When she hit the pavement, she got up and started to run, literally saved by a hair.

The truck had been a General Motors product, she thought, with a silver camper on top of it. The man? Probably in his late forties, with graying brown hair, what there was of it. He'd worn work clothes.

She considered that she had probably escaped death. And perhaps she had.

Still full of rage, living without a woman in Minneapolis, Harvey blamed the breakup of his marriage, the loss of his business, and his tenuous financial situation on Duane Homan and Billy Baughman. He was tremendously bitter, and he mooned over the memories of life with Alice as if she had indeed been the one great love of his life.

He wrote to her constantly, long, literate letters written in an astonishingly fine hand. The letters were addressed to Alice at their former home, which she now felt safe to inhabit. She also had her children living with her again. She was attempting to rebuild her life—without Harvey.

Also in Seattle, Mary Miller was trying to cope with the tragic changes in *her* life. The house that had been full of people yawned emptily now. Illness and age had claimed her grandmother and great-aunt, and Kathy was gone forever.

When Kathy's grandparents developed a roll of film that had been in their camera for a long time, they found that one frame had been of Kathy, a picture that no one remembered taking. Kathy gazed solemnly into the camera's lens, an almost invisible aura of light around her head. She held her white dog cuddled in her arms.

Mary had the picture enlarged and placed it on a shelf next to the fireplace, this last picture of her beautiful perfect daughter who would never be older than fifteen.

Mary tried to explain to her parents that the law was different in America, that the legal procedures they had mastered so long ago in Latvia had no weight in the United States. In Europe, a suspect is guilty until proved innocent. In America, it is just the opposite. The Purgalises shook their heads, unable to understand how Harvey Carignan was free to walk the streets when it seemed so likely that he had destroyed Kathy.

Mary herself had difficulty understanding.

"Can't he be extradited back from Minnesota?" she asked Homan. "Can he just run away like this?"

"We couldn't arrest him even if he comes back here," Duane Homan had told her. "We certainly have no legal way to go after him in Minnesota. We've written to warn the police in Minneapolis. That's all we can do."

Mary knew Homan and Billy Baughman well enough now

to see that the weight of the problem lay heavy on them too. She trusted them, and knew they shared her pain.

Kenny Miller found the loss of Kathy unbearable. He simply would not accept that Kathy was dead, murdered. He told his friends that Kathy had decided to get married and that she had moved after her wedding to another state. Privately, to Mary, he said that he knew someone had killed Kathy but that he couldn't say that out loud to his friends. She let his pathetic lies go; one day he would have to accept the truth, but if it helped him now to make up a story, so be it.

Kenny began to drag people home, other youngsters who seemed to have no place to go, even people he met on the street who appeared to need a warm meal and a place to sleep.

"I finally realized what he was trying to do," Mary recalls. "The house had been so full, and now it was so empty. He was trying to fill it up again. I had to tell him that we weren't the Union Gospel Mission, that no matter how many people he brought home, it would never be the same as it was."

Mary subscribed to two Minneapolis papers, determined to keep track of Harvey Carignan's whereabouts. Whenever the detectives heard anything, they reported it to her. But there was so little. Harvey was working in Minnesota; they didn't know if he would ever be back.

"One thing," Billy Baughman told her in the fall of 1973. "If Harvey should come back, we have a charge—not murder, but third-degree assault. His wife has finally agreed to file charges over a beating he gave her before she left him. If he shows up in Seattle, we can arrest him on that. But third-degree assault isn't enough to warrant extradition back here."

"And how long could you hold him?" Mary asked.

"Not long. Unless the parole board should decide to violate him on that charge. That's not likely, since he was on inactive parole."

Mary Miller plunged into volunteer work to help other victims' families. She had been active even before Kathy's disappearance in working for the rights of privacy regarding the sexual history of rape victims in courtroom testimony. Mary Miller was—and is—a mover and a shaker, ready to speak out when she sees inequities in the law. As the daughter of two judges, perhaps that was to be expected.

She had learned from her own experiences that there was nowhere bereaved families of crime victims could go for comfort and support. More than that, she vowed that the system had to be changed. The parole board had to assess early release of violent prisoners more carefully. They had to have all the information that was available on those prisoners' backgrounds when they made decisions that might well mean life or death.

Despite the loss of her daughter, Mary Miller was still a fighter. Her research revealed startling gaps in the prison and parole system; Harvey Carignan was only one of thousands of convicts released early from prison, even though their records were riddled with episodes of sexual violence. Now it appeared that Harvey had slipped through the system's cracks again. If Mary could do nothing else for Kathy, she would work to save someone else's child.

Mary still read the papers, focusing on crime stories. She found the names of other families who had experienced the tragedy of losing a child. Some of them had read of her loss and called her.

The first meeting of the embryo group that was to become the Families and Friends of Missing Persons and Violent Crime Victims took place in a West Seattle living room. Sally Peterson was there; Sally's five-year-old daughter, Heidi, had been kidnapped from the sidewalk in front of the family home. Eleven months after Heidi vanished, a heavy snowfall broke down some blackberry bushes in a vacant lot a block from the Peterson home—and revealed Heidi's skeleton. Duane Homan and Billy Baughman had been the primary investigators on Heidi's case too. And, again, they had homed in on a suspect, only to be blocked by the lack of physical evidence. That suspect would evade prosecution for almost a decade.

Lola Lindstad attended the first meeting. Lola's nineteen-year-old daughter, a new bride, had disappeared from her home on Thanksgiving Eve. Vonnie Stuth's body was discovered buried months later along the creek in back of a farm that had been rented by an escaped sex offender on the run from Michigan.

Doreen Hanson attended. Doreen's thirteen-year-old daughter, Janna, had been murdered by still another parolee. Her killer had committed suicide as he realized the police were closing in on him.

Something had to be done. It was as simple as that.

"I'd been to the legislature in Olympia before," Mary says. "Not all of our elected officials were amenable to change, but some of them would listen. We wanted those legislators to know what was happening. We wanted stricter laws on mandatory sentencing and parole. We were asking for someone to consider the victims of crimes, and the victims' families."

This small group would become the nucleus for a group with growing political clout throughout America, and Mary Miller would, in the fall of 1982, testify before President Reagan's Task Force on Victims' Rights as a widely recognized expert on that subject.

Quite possibly, her work with victims and their families saved her sanity. Such a strong woman, she had never buckled under before at what life had handed her, and she would not give in now, even when the worst possible thing that could happen to a mother had occurred.

While Mary restructured her life in Seattle, Harvey Carignan was feeling terribly sorry for himself in Minneapolis. He found a job in construction, but it didn't pay anywhere near what he had made in his own gas station. He stayed with his half-brother until he got a small stake, and then found an apartment.

And he wrote to Alice, the pleading letters manipulative in word and tone, blaming Alice for deserting him.

He wrote of the poignancy of their lives together, and chided Alice for looking at things without seeing "the true picture." His theme was always that Alice had rejected him and was unwilling to try to get along with him. He reminded her that he had offered to take her back, and painted himself as the spouse who was always ready to forgive and forget.

Harvey's correspondence was invariably full of the terrible problems that he dealt with, this poor soul all alone in Minneapolis. It cost him so much to furnish his apartment, he had been ripped off for double rent, and he had for some reason had to buy two complete new sets of tires for his car. He was making only $7.60 an hour, but he hastened to tell Alice that he was paying into a medical-insurance policy so that she and the children would be fully covered. It was another hook into Alice's conscience, although Harvey allowed that he knew the children were already covered by their father's insurance.

To add to Harvey's long streak of bad luck—or his assessment of his life that way—he wrote in the fall of 1973 that he had been the victim of a savage attack.

He said that he had gone to downtown Minneapolis, where he had been beaten and robbed by "two white girls, a black girl, and two black men." They had used a claw hammer in their attack on him, and Harvey reported that he had suffered severe injuries, including four huge lumps on his head, the near-loss of the upper part of his right ear, and the dread possibility that he might lose his right eye. He said that he had no money, no job, and that he didn't know how long it would be before he could even work again.

If the assault actually happened, Harvey did not report it to the Minneapolis police.

Anyone reading Harvey's letters to his estranged wife without knowing about his background might have mistaken him for a tenderhearted saint. He wrote of watching a television show with his nieces and nephews; the children's reactions to the sight of a "roadrunner killing a sidewinder" had sickened him. He had actually become nauseated, he told Alice, to see the youngsters laughing and pointing at the snake in its death convulsions. He could not imagine how anyone could "so intensely enjoy the sight of killing." He had been driven from the house to a tavern, where he consumed beer and chili to calm himself. That, he wrote his estranged wife, had been a mistake. The beer, the chili, and the clatter of radiators turning on in the dark recesses of his apartment had given him horrible nightmares about murder. He had wakened in a terrible fright.

A most sensitive man.

Harvey assured Alice that he was absolutely opposed to violence of any kind. He begged her to believe that despite certain occurrences which might seem to indicate otherwise, he had never in his life intentionally hurt anything or anyone.

Alice would have liked to believe him. His love letters were getting to her, and she sometimes longed to have him back. And then her doubts crept back in. She was still afraid of him.

On Sunday, September 9, 1973, thirteen-year-old Jerri Billings of Duluth, Minnesota, was hitchhiking in the northeastern section of Minneapolis. Jerri had run away from home a short time before and moved into an apartment in northeast Minneapolis with a girlfriend and several young men. On September 9 she was headed to a boyfriend's apartment by the only means of transportation she had: hitchhiking. She had obtained a ride part of the way, and held her thumb out again on the corner of Lowry Avenue and Central Avenue N.E.

When a pickup truck with a silver canopy on top slowed down and then stopped and backed up, she ran happily to climb in.

The driver was a big man who looked to be between forty-five and fifty. He smiled at her and told her he would take her wherever she needed to go. She thought him a strange-looking man; he had such an odd-shaped forehead that ended in a kind of peak on top of his bald head, but he seemed nice enough. He wore green work clothes and heavy work boots.

"My name is Paul," he said. "What's yours?"

She gave him a false name. She was on the run, and she didn't want anyone to know her real name. She didn't want her mother to find her.

Jerri jabbered at the driver, giving him the address of her destination again, and he nodded. But as they drove along, she realized he was going in the wrong direction. He was heading out into the country, away from the city.

When she started to protest, the man only grunted and kept on driving. They were going too fast for her to jump out. Before she could say anything else, the man unzipped his trousers and used his free hand to force Jerri's head down toward his penis. She tried to squirm away, but he was terribly strong and he was hurting her neck. In crude terms, he ordered her to perform oral sodomy on him.

Nauseated, she complied.

After a long time, he let her sit up and she could see they were way out in the country, racing along a highway.

"Take your jeans down," he commanded.

When she had done this, he ordered her to lower her panties. And then she felt his hand between her legs. He held a claw hammer in his fist, and she was terrified when she realized that the man was pushing the handle of the hammer inside of her, moving it up and down as if it were a male sex organ.

"Now, give me a blow-job again," he growled.

Her head was pushed down over his penis again, and his organ was forced into her mouth while he continued to jam the hammer into her vagina. When she gagged, his fingers closed tightly around the back of her neck.

She felt hopeless. No one could see her from cars passing by, and the pickup truck was taking them farther and farther into the country, where corn grew six feet high on each side of the road.

Jerri fought to lift her head and felt a tremendous blow. Her head seemed to explode and she saw flashing lights. He had hit her with the hammer.

She started to cry and the man told her to shut up. Whimpering, she crouched against the seat. She tried to memorize what the truck cab looked like, although she doubted she would ever get a chance to tell anyone about it. There were two bucket seats, and a board rested between them.

After they had driven for a long time, the man turned the truck into a cornfield and stopped.

"Get out."

She hesitated, and he picked her up in his arms and carried

her into the field, so far that she knew they could not possibly be seen from the country road.

The big man dropped her to the ground on her stomach. She could hear him fumbling with his trousers, and then she felt a searing pain. He was attempting to rape her, but it wasn't normal. He was trying to enter her from behind, through her rectum. She screamed and pleaded, and the man finally gave up trying to penetrate her that way.

He yanked her by the hair until she was in a kneeling position, and then forced his penis into her mouth again. When he had ejaculated, he pushed her away and told her to get dressed.

Jerri Billings had fully expected that the man would kill her, but he allowed her to get dressed and then he walked her back to his truck. He drove without speaking until they reached Crystal, a small suburban town northwest of Minneapolis. Abruptly he stopped the truck.

"Get out, and don't tell anyone . . . ever."

Jerri ran, not looking back, as she heard the truck's motor gun and the tires squeal as the man drove off.

Jerry Billings had run away from home; she couldn't go back now. And she couldn't call the police and report what had happened to her or else they would arrest her too. At least, that's what she thought would happen. She hid until she was sure the man was gone for good, and told herself that she must never tell. What had happened to her was so awful she couldn't imagine telling anyone about it anyway, certainly not a male police officer.

Her head hurt where he'd hit her with the hammer, and she was sick to her stomach from the other, but she wasn't really hurt. She wasn't dead, and she'd thoroughly expected that she was going to be.

Jerri stayed away from home two more days, but the memory of what had happened to her was so terrifying that she was afraid to be on the streets. She went home. She didn't tell her mother about the rape, and her mother told her she was fed up with her running away. Jerri was immediately placed under the jurisdiction of the St. Louis County Juvenile Court as a habitual runaway.

She stayed in detention until October 2, and then she was admitted to the Red Wing Training School.

In a way, a circle had been completed. The man who had sodomized Jerri Billings had spent his teen years in a training school; now his latest victim had been committed to one.

The dark-haired youngster didn't tell anyone what had happened to her. She had nightmares, and no one understood why, and she seemed afraid of shadows, but no one asked her what was wrong and she didn't volunteer. She did vow never, never to hitchhike again.

On October 29, 1973, Jerri could not bear to keep the attack secret any longer. She reported it to the Goodhue County Sheriff's Office in Red Wing, Minnesota. She felt she had to report it; she thought she'd seen the man who attacked her at a church service at the state training school.

The Red Wing Police Department initiated an investigation along with the Goodhue Sheriff's Office. During this probe, Jerri was given a polygraph examination, which indicated she was telling the truth about her abduction. However, detectives could not develop sufficient probable cause to arrest the man Jerri had seen at the church service. Jerri was able to say only that the man "looked like the man who attacked me."

In February 1974 the case was turned over to the Hennepin County Sheriff's Office in Minneapolis, because the original abduction had occurred in their jurisdiction. That office continued the investigation, but no one was convinced that the man Jerri had seen at the church service was actually the man who had attacked her. With the press of other cases, the attack on Jerri was put on a back burner.

Throughout the summer of 1973, Duane Homan and Billy Baughman had sought clues that might tie Harvey into Kathy Miller's murder. The probe continued to be frustrating. However, on October 30, 1973, the man who had given them the roll of black Visqueen (the roll which proved unmatchable) called again. "I've found another section of that plastic," he reported. "When I went to mount my daughter's snow tires, I found there was some plastic in the trunk of her car. It's the same stuff. It's possible that this is the missing link. The plastic I gave Harvey could have been torn off just before I gave some to my daughter.''

Homan and Baughman drove at once to the man's home and retrieved this missing section. They took it to the crime lab for comparison with the piece that had been wrapped around Kathy's body when it was found.

"We played jigsaw puzzle," Homan recalls. "We were sure that this was the piece with the edges that would match, but we turned it sideways, upside down, crossways. We spent four days in the crime lab trying to find the matching edges. We practically stood on our heads to make that section match . . . and then we had to admit that it didn't match. It was exactly the same lot of Visqueen, just like the other sample had been—but there was a piece missing somewhere.''

The two detectives were monitoring Harvey's location by checking motor-vehicle registration in Minnesota and by talking to Alice Carignan from time to time. She told them about Harvey's letters and phone calls begging her to come back to him. She had resisted his entreaties so far, but still she hadn't been able to bring herself to file for divorce. Harvey's address that fall was North Fremont Street in Minneapolis, his brother's home.

Harvey Carignan continued to inundate his lost wife with mail. When she did not answer immediately, he was bereft, convinced that the mails had gone astray. He felt his prose was so persuasive that she would surely respond to him if she had read his letters. He told her that he was finding it harder, day by day, to go on without her. When he was not working, the empty days and the lack of money to distract him from thoughts of her were almost more than he could bear.

Alice was a little perplexed; Harvey now remembered their marriage as one long honeymoon, filled with love. He blamed her for wasting that love and for turning it into "an ugly and grotesque monster causing heartache and pain." *She* still remembered moments that weren't so idyllic, the times he'd blacked her eyes and cut her face up with angry blows. When Harvey talked of the "loving violence" of their passion, she wondered just what he meant.

By January 1974 Harvey's love seemed to have grown

even stronger. He wrote that he had had no other woman, because no other woman could match Alice.

He did occasionally visit a restaurant where he nursed a beer and verbally taunted one of the waitresses—also named Alice. The woman thought him a bit off the wall, and asked him why he bothered to sit in her section when he obviously didn't like her. He gave her only an oblique answer. He told her that he just liked to hear people say the name "Alice."

Perhaps to pick at some jealousy in Alice, Harvey sometimes wrote about attractive women he encountered. Although he always stressed his fidelity to her, he extolled the beauties of other women, and on one occasion he betrayed his fascination with very young women.

He had gone to a bar for some beers and to discuss the Super Bowl with some of the regulars. A "wondrously beautiful" young girl had come in with two young men to shoot pool. Harvey was absolutely entranced with her, but he hastened to explain to Alice that it was only because she was such a superb pool player.

Harvey Carignan had never been a social animal, and he was becoming more and more isolated and increasingly introspective. During the first cold winter in Minneapolis, he considered himself a loner. It pleased him to sit back and observe others and to realize that he was so superior to them intellectually.

He began to play head games with the people he met in bars. They were not friends; he'd never had friends. He enjoyed the reaction he got when he stared off into space vacantly in the middle of a conversation. The discomfiture of the other person was fuel for his ego. After he'd pulled the vacant-stare routine, he would simply walk away. People shook their heads and wondered why the thread of conversation had unraveled.

He wrote Alice that he delighted in keeping other people just a shade off-balance. They were such fools. The limited mentality of most of the people he met bored him. He had become adept at hiding his contempt for their ignorance. But he was pleased, even conceited, that they obviously found him brilliant.

And yet, although he sensed that they admired his intelligence, he also deduced that his companions felt he was not superior in any area that mattered. He knew they laughed at him and found him a rather odd duck.

The mind games became "a serious game—as war is a game." Despite his protestations of superiority, Harvey admitted to Alice that he was constantly being humiliated by the barbs of the idiots who hung out at the taverns. He considered that he had a "satirical sense of humor" because he had a knack for remarks that flew like arrows to his targets' weakest spots.

He had mistaken "satirical" for "sadistic."

He bragged that he had hurt some people badly with his unerring aim with cutting words. And, of course, their dislike for him increased with each new insult. Their responses to him "humiliated me more." And so he responded with more taunts.

Although Harvey Carignan purported to want friends and acceptance, he actually preferred the rush that came when he teased people—the overweight women, and the old men, and the insecure divorcées, and the others who came to the tavern to lose themselves in a blur of alcohol—to any warmth of friendship.

He claimed in his letters to Alice that he wished he could change places with those he ridiculed—even the dullest clods—but that he could not take life's humiliations without erupting into anger. He could not forgive, nor could he forget what had been done to him in his life. He could not accept a gentle jest without returning it with a verbal punch to the gut.

Harvey's introspection is interesting to contemplate; he could apparently search his personality and bring out certain truths, but then his perception became flawed. His rage took over and left no room at all for the feelings of others. It had always been that way. The world was against him. He deserved attention and love; no one else did.

Harvey was not stupid. He was clever, verbal, literate, and deviously manipulative. He could weave words into traps, manufacture false truths from whole cloth, and then cover his tracks until they might never have crushed the earth beneath his feet.

Time and time again Harvey wrote of one of the constant needs in his life—"a passion for certainty."

"I have an unhappy passion for certainty. I must be doubly and triply sure of everything."

A passion for certainty. An odd and ambiguous term. He needed to be certain that Alice still loved him and would one day return. He needed to know that all aspects of his life were well-organized, all of his secret thoughts and deeds pigeonholed where only he could retrieve them. And so he kept records, notations that meant something special to him on papers hidden in odd places, records in his head.

Death might be considered the ultimate certainty. Unchanging and unchangeable. Had Harvey satisfied his passion for certainty by stopping the lives of females who did not want him?

Even though Harvey's letters and phone calls had been masterpieces of manipulation, Alice had not responded as he expected she would. He had written that her son needed him as a father, completely overlooking the beatings he'd administered to the boy. He had painted a glowing picture of what their lives would be like, but Alice was dragging her feet. She answered his letters, sending one back for ten of his, but she would not come to him.

It occurred to him that Alice might possibly be holding back because of the occasional beating he'd given her; Harvey spelled out the terms that would prevent any further rough stuff. All Alice had to remember was that he would never hit her again—unless she should go to bed with another man while she was still legally married to him. He allowed that, even then, he might not hit her. He might and he might not.

He accused Alice of "seeing dragons that don't exist," explaining that he was actually a good person if only given the chance. Other people were telling Alice lies and distorted truths about him, he argued, and he begged her to try to understand the meaning of their words in the proper context.

"Alice, I am the same person now as I was then. I haven't changed a bit."

And he had not changed. Not a bit.

Although Harvey had pledged his undying love over and over again to Alice, and warned her of what might happen if she were unfaithful to him, he met another woman in January 1974—a woman to whom he was strongly attracted.

Harvey was on his way home late on the bitterly cold evening when a car ahead of him stalled. He saw that there were three women in it. He pulled his truck up behind them and approached the driver. One of the women was, in Harvey's words, "a little old lady," but the other two were younger, and the youngest was very pretty. Harvey offered his assistance.

The ladies in distress happened to be Jehovah's Witnesses, out doing "God's work." The temperature on that January night was twenty-four degrees below zero and still dropping, and there were no service stations in sight. The three women considered Harvey's offer a beneficence from God himself. He explained that they had apparently broken the universal joint on their car, and that it wasn't something that could be fixed there on the street. When he graciously offered to give them a lift home, they accepted.

It was a long trip; the women lived in Anoka, a suburb some distance away, and Harvey chatted with his passengers. He judged two of them to be "idiotic" and fanatical," but he maintained his chivalrous attitude. By an odd coincidence, one of the women had lived in Seattle for a time, and had known Alice when she was married to her first husband. All of the women thought Harvey charming, and thanked him profusely when he delivered them safely to their homes.

Harvey wrote to Alice about the incident, using it to show her that he was, indeed, a pretty nice guy. He stressed that he'd found all the stranded women boring, and that their religious fervor had turned him off.

In truth, however, one of the "religious fanatics" did appeal to him. Her name was Eileen Hunley, she was twenty-eight years old but appeared to be much younger, and Harvey would follow up on his interest in her within weeks.

But first he had to try one more time to win Alice back. He

put Eileen in the back part of his mind; should he find himself alone without a woman to love and comfort him, Eileen might just fill the bill.

In February 1974 Harvey decided that he would have to confront Alice in person to win her back. On February 27 Homan and Baughman were notified that Harvey's car had been seen back in Seattle—at 180th and 15th N.E. They notified the Tact Squad immediately, and word came back that Harvey had been arrested on the third-degree-assault warrant filed by Alice because of her split lip and blackened eyes.

He was brought into the station and Homan and Baughman questioned him. Face to face again after eight months, all three men were tense.

"Harvey," Baughman said slowly, "you're in here because of the charges filed by your wife, but you're still our main suspect in Kathy Miller's death. We aren't going to rest until it's solved—one way or another."

Harvey glared at them. "From the first, I've felt you've picked on me, zeroed in on me. However, after the twentieth-hand reports that I've received, I'd have to say you were doing a good job." He relaxed and smiled.

They studied him, and took his remarks to mean that whatever circumstantial evidence they had come up with, he knew they couldn't prove anything against him. He was almost enjoying the standoff.

Harvey still refused to take a lie-detector test.

"If you take the polygraph, and pass it," Homan said, "we'll certainly go in another direction. Until that time, you are our suspect, and you were the last person, we think, to see Kathy alive."

Harvey began to sweat, and his features began to twitch the way they always had when the detectives probed too closely.

Harvey took another tack; he asked the detectives to think about their families, their wives and children, and try to understand his position, that of a man who only wanted what they had, a loving wife and children.

And then Harvey smiled triumphantly and played his ace.

"I only got back in the city yesterday, and I went directly

to Alice. We made love. She's not going to press the charges against me on the assault."

They had almost expected it. Alice vacillated constantly when it came to Harvey.

"We're still going to fingerprint you, photograph you, and process you through the jail," Billy Baughman told him.

"Be my guest."

Jean Battista, the fingerprint technician, reported later, however, that Harvey would not sign the fingerprint card. "He thought I took too many, especially his palm prints—just for a third-degree-assault case."

Harvey didn't look good. He'd lost considerable weight, and he seemed on the fine edge of exhaustion. Still, he had regained his bravado. He figured he'd beaten the detectives he hated so much, and it gave him confidence.

"I'm an old-timer," Carignan bragged. "I've spent twenty-seven years inside the walls, and I'm never going back."

Just as Harvey had predicted, Alice came in to say she was dropping the assault charges against him. Her daughter, Georgia, had accompanied her to the Homicide offices, and she broke down in tears when she heard that her mother had backed down and was seriously considering going back to Minnesota with him.

"I'm afraid for her," the girl sobbed. "I don't want her to go back there with him, but there's nothing I can do about it. She won't listen to me."

11

Somehow, common sense prevailed with Alice Carignan; she remained in Seattle, and Harvey left without her. He resumed his crusade by mail.

He beseeched her to refrain from sexual relations with other men and told her of his haunting wish that she would still one day return to him.

Alice had suggested that they remain good friends, but Harvey wrote that they were actually "poor tormented lovers, with a love as great as Abelard and Heloise, Antony and Cleopatra, and Romeo and Juliet." He proclaimed that their romance was just as tragic as any of the blighted affairs recorded down through history. Of course, it was not his fault. Alice was at fault because she did not have the courage to join him in Minneapolis, and he clearly couldn't return to Seattle, no matter how much he burned for her.

He could not come back to Seattle without facing another confrontation with Duane Homan and Billy Baughman, and they had begun to get under his skin. They knew nothing certain, of course, but they nagged at him and kept up with their questions. He couldn't understand their tenacity. They didn't know that the game was over; they didn't know when to quit.

He tried to explain to Alice why he had had to run once again back to Minnesota.

"There were people watching me, people praying I'd do just one little wrong thing so they could crush me, or even kill me. People who can't stand to be wrong; people who with malice and perfidy have tried to ruin me for something I didn't do, people who have convinced themselves I am wrong and they are right, people who could murder me in cold blood to prove they are right, and I am wrong, two men who would do anything to prove a case they fabricated in their vicious and twisted minds. I was afraid to die that day. I had to leave. . . . Everything that was done to me was done with malice, lies, and twisting truths until they too became lies."

The two "villains" possessed of "vicious and twisted minds" were, of course, Billy Baughman and Duane Homan. It was true that they continued on Harvey's case, although the chance of arresting him for Kathy Miller's murder now seemed a lost cause. Their quarry still walked free, although thousands of miles away. As long as he was free, they dreaded the very real possibility that his toll would mount. They knew there was nothing left for them to do to prevent it.

All through the snowy days in Minneapolis in the spring of 1974, Harvey continued his campaign to get Alice back. But he was getting worried; she had hinted that she was considering marrying someone else. He wrote to her continually, dredging up the most romantic phrases he could find.

On Easter Sunday he wrote to remind her that the next day would be their second anniversary. He accused Alice of tearing apart their marriage, and likened her action to someone who desecrated a beautiful painting or who deliberately ripped the petals from an exquisite flower. He warned her that she would only find heartbreak if she considered yet a third marriage. They had had only a few "bad moments," after all.

Alice was not swayed; she remembered the few "bad moments" more vividly, apparently, than Harvey did.

Convinced, finally, that Alice wasn't coming back to him, Harvey Carignan broke his vow to remain faithful to the wife who continued to reject his offers to rejoin him. "Abelard" abandoned "Heloise" as a lost cause, and sought female companionship.

*   *   *

Eileen Hunley was, like Alice, a most unworldly woman. She was a native of Kansas, and she had moved to Minneapolis from Kansas City in March 1973. She had found a job working in a day-care center. She would be Harvey's next woman.

When Harvey called her, she remembered, of course, the kind man who had given her and her friends a ride on the frigid night in January. He had seemed a perfect gentleman—driving miles out of his way to help ladies in trouble. Even her elderly friend had commented that Harvey "didn't seem a bad sort for being a Roman Catholic." He was, at least, a Christian, and Eileen thought that was what mattered.

Eileen might have seemed a strange choice for Harvey. But then, Harvey hadn't met many women since he'd gone back to Minnesota, and Eileen seemed more receptive than most. She was a pretty, dark-haired woman, very religious and very involved in "The Way," a fundamentalist church group that leaned heavily on literal translation of the Old Testament for its doctrine. When Eileen met Harvey, he seemed lost—a man who could benefit from the teachings of "The Way," and she gladly introduced him to the membership.

In a way, dating Harvey might be considered "God's work"; if Eileen denied her sexual attraction to him, that was only because she had long had trouble dealing with her own sexuality. Her religious advisers had never wanted to discuss sex or her feelings in that direction. Harvey *was* a passionate man, but he also seemed a reverent man.

Harvey had read the Bible during his long years in the joint, and although he had not evinced much interest in religion during his Seattle years, he would later claim that his faith had been strong for a long time.

Eileen and Harvey began a very close relationship in May 1974, so close that she was thrilled when he said he'd like to drive her to Kansas to meet her family. In the third week of June, they journeyed to Goessel, Kansas. While Harvey was still given to night driving by himself, and left Goessel for periods during the visit, it was, all in all, successful in Eileen's mind.

They maintained their relationship through the first part of the summer.

Eileen didn't seem to mind that Harvey's financial situation was precarious. Actually, she felt sorry for him, and knew he was trying to turn his life around by joining "The Way." He told her of his problems with a former landlady. When he couldn't come up with the rent, the landlady had kicked him out and kept all of his belongings. She had told him that she would pack his things up and give them to him, but she never had and she wouldn't allow him to come in and do it.

He'd rented a new place for a hundred and twenty dollars a month, but he'd had to buy a bed, a table and chairs, a dresser, and new silverware. His new place was really only a room, but it was pleasant, and he kept it immaculate. He seemed to be such a proud man, and he was trying so hard.

Eileen knew he'd had some rough times in the past, but she did not know the extent of his prison life, nor did she know about the investigation that had sent him fleeing from Seattle.

Eileen had wanted a good, religious man, and she certainly seemed to have found a devout follower of the Lord when she found Harvey.

With Eileen's entrance into Harvey's life, the storm of letters back to Seattle slowed to a trickle and then stopped entirely. Eileen wanted Harvey, and Alice didn't.

Alice felt ambivalent; in a way, she was relieved that it was over. In another way, she missed his love letters.

Soon the questions that had nagged at Alice fell squarely on Eileen. Sometimes she wondered if Harvey was all he claimed to be.

Things started to go sour in July. Harvey showed signs of temper that startled her. He also seemed to have a great thirst for alcohol, a propensity that warred with Eileen's faith. As she understood it, God intended man's body to be a temple and not to be profaned with excess. When she mentioned her concerns to Harvey, he was enraged.

Disillusioned, Eileen—like the women who had come before her—realized she had made a terrible mistake. Eileen, however, paid more dearly for her mistake than Sheila and Alice had.

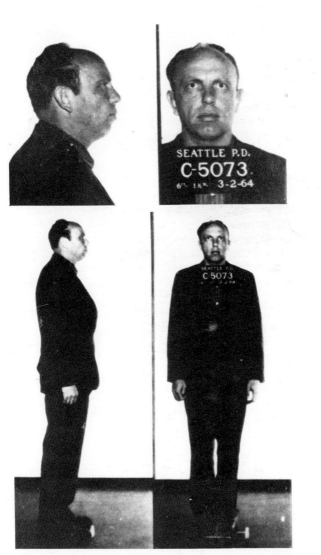

Thickly muscled Harvey Carignan was arrested for second-degree burglary in 1964. Sentenced to fifteen years in prison, he was released four years later. His police record noted that he was "capable of superhuman strength."

In May 1972, Seattle teenager Kathy Sue Miller answered an ad for a job in a gas station and was never seen alive again.

Homicide detectives Billy Baughman (above) and Duane Homan (below) of the Seattle Police Department pursued Kathy Sue Miller's killer.

Detective Baughman, at right, searches for evidence at a plywood mill. He broke his ankle while climbing over piles of logs.

Harvey Carignan, under police surveillance, at work in his gas station. This photo was taken less than a week after Kathy Sue Miller's disappearance.

The lonely road leading into the Tulalip Indian Reservation, where Kathy Sue Miller's body was found.

The body site.

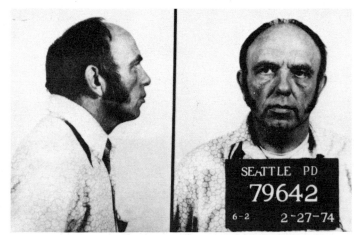

In 1974, Detectives Baughman and Homan arrested Carignan on charges of assaulting his ex-wife. When she dropped the charges, Carignan was released and went to Minneapolis.

Jean Battista, a Seattle Police Criminalist, dusts Carignan's car for fingerprints.

A tire track found near the scene of a murder in Minnesota was later found to match Carignan's car, the purple Toronado.

Archie Sonenstahl, Hennepin County, Minnesota, sheriff's detective, linked Carignan to a series of brutal attacks on women in his district.

Eileen told Harvey that she didn't want to see him anymore. She knew that she would see him in church, and she told him that she hoped they could be friends. Her words reminded him of Alice's rejection.

Eileen was seen by friends in her home at 1408 Spruce Street in Minneapolis on the muggy, hot Saturday of August 10, 1974. She did not attend church the next day, or appear for a prayer meeting at "The Way." Nor did she report for work at the day-care center on Monday.

In fact, no one ever saw Eileen Hunley alive again.

Her employers at the child-care center worried about her, and they worried more when Harvey Carignan showed up at the center and said he had been sent to collect Eileen's most recent paycheck. They refused to give him the check meant for Eileen, despite his story that she was indisposed and had sent him to retrieve her pay for her.

Eileen's apartment had been left as if she had only just stepped away from it; all of her belongings were there, everything that surely would mean something to her. Her family in Kansas had not heard from her. No one had heard from her.

It was incomprehensible that a young woman as dependable and as devout as Eileen Hunley should simply turn her back on her life and responsibilities and walk away.

As the search for Eileen went on in the Minneapolis area throughout August and into September, local law-enforcement authorities could not predict that a virtual hurricane of violence was about to descend over their territory.

On September 8, a Sunday, June Lynch, one day short of her seventeenth birthday, was hitchhiking with a friend, Lisa King, sixteen, on Lake Street in Minneapolis. Lisa and June, students at an alternative school—the Work Opportunity Center on Colfax and West Lake—got into a green Chevrolet sedan that stopped for them. The driver was an older man, well over forty, and he was balding.

"Girls," he said, "if you're not in a big hurry to get where you're going, you can make twenty-five dollars."

"How?" June asked suspiciously.

"My son's truck ran out of gas up in Mora and I want to get it back to Minneapolis, but I need a driver to bring it down. If either of you have a license, I could take you up there and follow you back. Wouldn't take that long and I'd pay you twenty-five bucks."

It sounded like a lot of money just for driving a truck, and the girls agreed to help. The driver turned his car north and headed for Mora.

But he stopped before he reached the outskirts of Mora and turned into a lonely wooded area. When he got out of the car, the girls could see what a truly big man he was. He reached back to take a hammer, a screwdriver, and a five-gallon gas can from his car.

"You . . ." he directed Lisa. "You stay in the car, and your friend can come with me and get my kid's truck started."

June followed the man into the woods, wondering why in the world the truck would be stashed way back in the deepest part of the forest. The bald man was in front of her, and then he was suddenly turning toward her and raising his hand with something clutched in it.

She had time to scream, and then her eyes could focus on nothing but thick black smoke, and she fell. Lisa heard June scream, and ran back into the trees where she'd seen June disappear. Her friend was on the ground, bleeding profusely from the head. The man was gone.

Lisa found help at a farmhouse, and a deputy sheriff was summoned. June regained consciousness in the backseat of the deputy's speeding patrol car. She had no idea why the man had hit her with the hammer. She hadn't said anything to annoy him.

Emergency-room physicians found that June had been struck on the head seven times with a hammer. She had suffered a severe concussion, but except for a pounding headache and dizzy spells for weeks, she would be all right.

Six days later, on the morning of September 14, Gwen Burton, nineteen, had the great misfortune of meeting the angry man who roved at will through the Minneapolis area.

Gwen, a student nurse at the Abbott-Northwestern Nursing School, was pretty and petite, with short dark hair curling around her face. On September 14 she had a problem. Her blue Ford was parked near the Sears parking lot at Chicago and Lake streets in Minneapolis and she could not get the engine to turn over. As she stood peering worriedly at the jumble of wires and parts under the hood, a green Chevrolet Caprice pulled up beside her. The driver was a middle-aged man dressed in green work clothes, partially bald, with a deeply furrowed face.

"Trouble?" he asked as he stepped beside her to look under the hood."

"It won't start. I don't know what's wrong with it."

The man fiddled with something under the hood, and then looked over at her. "I can fix it—but not without my tools. We'll run on over to my place and get them."

"I don't have any money to pay you," Gwen said. "I just bought a present in Sears, and that took most of my cash."

This didn't seem to bother the big man. Without speaking, he rolled up her windows, closed the hood, and led her by the elbow to his car.

He held the passenger door of his car open and indicated that Gwen should get in. She hesitated; she really wanted—needed—her car, but she didn't know the man. As she pulled back unconsciously, he frowned at her. More than a frown—an angry grimace.

"I said *get in*."

Gwen looked around the parking lot and saw that they were alone. She was frightened. Her hesitancy seemed to enrage the man. She stood frozen, and the man's fingers on her arm tightened as he pushed her into his car.

As the car pulled out, she was more frightened. She should have stood her ground, but his anger had had an almost hypnotic power. He seemed calmer now as he shifted into high gear and jammed his foot on the accelerator. He drove rapidly away from the city, heading southwest toward Chaska, Minnesota.

"Where do you live?" Gwen asked timidly.

"Out here a ways," he answered.

She saw that they had passed over the Hennepin County line and were in a rural area of Carver County. Much too far.

Why would any man be such a Good Samaritan that he would drive this far to pick up tools to fix a stranger's car?

She found out a moment later when the Chevy turned onto a gravel road. The big man turned toward her and said, "Slide over and sit by me."

She shook her head.

"You know, I'm an expert in judo and karate. Come on over and sit by me. My wife and I aren't getting along well—"

"No."

"I'll pay you—you said you were short on money. I'll pay you thirty dollars a week if you'll . . . meet with me. I could make a hooker out of you."

She heard her own voice, softened to a whisper by fear. "I don't want to sit by you. I want you to take me back to my car or let me out here. I'll get my own ride back."

One of his beefy hands darted out and grabbed her hair, pulling her forcefully across the seat toward him. "Come here, bitch!"

Gwen fought the stranger, but she was as effective as a kitten fighting a gorilla. She was sure he could kill her with one swipe of his hand, and she wanted to live.

It was clear what he wanted; he was forcing her head over his groin and demanding that she fellate him. She decided that she had to comply to save her life. It went on for such a long time, but he apparently wasn't satisfied.

The huge man ripped at the waist of her jeans and pulled them off, taking her panties with them. When she struggled, she felt his hands close around her throat. She passed out. Each time she fought back to consciousness, he choked her again. Once. Twice. Three times. She knew that she was probably going to die. She could not help crying, and that made him angry. He slapped her in the face with his open hand.

When she came to the next time, surprised that she was still alive, she found herself sitting on a blue plaid blanket spread out on the ground. He demanded oral sex again, yanking her to her knees. While she fellated him again, he inserted the handle of a claw hammer into her vagina, jamming it into the soft tissues viciously. She felt something break inside of her; her hymen had been pierced with a wooden bludgeon, and she felt herself hemorrhage.

"I like to see you suffer," he told her, and she could tell he was relishing her pain.

"You're going to kill me, aren't you?" she asked hopelessly.

He smiled—an ugly smile. "You shouldn't say things like that. You'll give me ideas."

Oh, God. She shouldn't have said that. That made it too real, saying it out loud. Maybe he hadn't thought of it before, but she knew he liked the idea.

He seemed to enjoy playing with her, reveling in her total helplessness.

Twice his fist thudded into her stomach, knocking her breath out of her and making her double over with pain.

He moved behind her and she turned around. She saw him moving behind the car, and then she saw the claw hammer in his hand.

"Please . . . no!"

"Now I am going to kill you, you whore."

The hammer came crashing down on her skull, and she crumpled. Her last thought was that she was dying.

A long time later, Gwen woke up. She was lying in a gully in a pool of something wet. When she could focus her eyes, she saw that the pool was red, a spreading circle of her own blood. She touched her hair and found it full of dried blood, and beneath it, fresh blood still oozed, draining her life away.

Her head hurt so terribly, and she was weaker than she had ever been, so weak that she could barely move. Her first thought was that she would lie back down and go to sleep.

"I saw no reason to get up," she would tell detectives later. "It was easier to lie down and let myself die."

And then she remembered that her sister had called her that morning with wonderful news. Her sister had just found out that she was pregnant.

"I thought that if I died I would never get to see that baby. I had to live; I had to find somebody who would help me."

She listened for sounds that would indicate her attacker

was still waiting nearby, waiting to finish killing her. But she heard nothing but the raucous cries of crows. He was gone. She had to believe he was gone. If she waited any longer, she would surely bleed to death.

Gwen stood up, but her legs would not support her and she fell heavily back into the bottom of the gully. Oddly, she felt no pain at all now, only a leaden heaviness that seemed to drag her body back to earth.

It took her three tries to get out of the six-foot-deep gully. She would make it to the top and then feel herself sliding and tumbling back to the bottom. If she stayed there, hidden from anyone, she would certainly die. With tremendous force of will she managed to crawl up to the top once more. She rested for several minutes and then heaved herself out and onto the dirt of an alfalfa field.

She looked around, and her heart sank. The field was huge, and there was no one anywhere. Far off, beyond this field and another one, through a small woods, she could see a road. She estimated that it was a quarter of a mile away, perhaps farther. It seemed an impossible task to reach the road.

Gwen did not try to stand again. Rather, she crawled on her belly across the field's furrows, through the stubble of harvested crops. She had no idea what time it was. It had been late morning when the man forced her into his car, but now the sun was lowering in the sky.

She would crawl awhile, and then rest, exhausted from the effort. She made it across the first field and saw that there was a barbed-wire fence separating it from the field that abutted the road. Oblivious of the deep scratches the wire made in her arms and legs, she managed to drag herself across the fence, and fell like a stone into the next field.

Her watch told her that it had taken her more than two hours to traverse the first field. Now she could hear cars rushing by, the rumbling tires of tractors going from one farm to another. She screamed, but the wind caught her voice and swallowed it. The cars on the road didn't even slow down.

No one could hear her.

She began to crawl again, clutching at the earth with her hands and then pulling her body along. Three and a half hours after she'd dragged herself out of the gully, she reached the roadside, but she was far too weak to stand up and signal for help.

"Every time a car or tractor would go by," she would say much later, "I'd wave and try to yell. But my voice was too weak. My jaw hurt from trying to open my mouth."

Several times, when she waved desperately, cars slowed down, and the occupants stared at her. And only returned her wave! Did they think she was lying in the grass beside the road sunbathing? What was the matter with people? Couldn't they see that she was injured?

Apparently not.

It would be dark soon, and the chill of a Minnesota fall evening would creep over the field. She knew she would not live until morning, and debated trying to crawl out into the middle of the gravel road, where a car would have to stop—if the driver could see her in time.

Her grip on reality came and went, and it would be easy now to give in to the lassitude that paralyzed her limbs, and let herself slip into endless sleep. But she had come so far; she wasn't going to die now.

Just as she reached the limits of desperation, she heard a tractor approaching, and she called out one more time. She heard the tractor motor slow, and then saw a farmboy running toward her.

Gwen Burton was rushed to Abbott Hospital, where doctors found her to be in critical condition. She had lost quantities of blood and she had a depressed skull fracture.

Immediate surgery was necessary to reduce the fracture before her brain swelled and macerated itself against the unyielding skull above it. The surgery lasted for several hours. Surgeons found that she had a circle-shaped skull fracture, the circle of bone driven a full inch into the left brain itself. Painstakingly they picked bone fragments from brain tissue.

The prognosis was guarded. If the steroids they had administered worked, and if the brain did not now swell profoundly, and if she did not develop an infection, she might live.

Gwen Burton did live, but she would be partially paralyzed in her right arm and leg for months. Her ability to concentrate would be compromised, her balance would be unstable, and when she was tired, words would not come. She was forced to drop out of nursing school. Before the attack, Gwen had been a swimmer, a skier, and a member of a girls' football team. She would no longer be able to participate in any of these sports.

She had also been a virgin. Although she had not been raped with a male penis, it would be a long time—if ever—before she could consider sex anything but a violation of her person.

There was a pattern emerging, although the balding man with a rage against women was clever. The attacks had taken place in different jurisdictions; it gave him a head start while detectives in many different offices sorted out their cases. Jerri Billings had been picked up in Minneapolis and taken to a cornfield in the north part of Hennepin County, and then released in Crystal. June Lynch and Lisa King had been driven close to Mora, Minnesota, in Kanabec County, and Gwen Burton had been taken from Minneapolis into rural Carver County. And Eileen Hunley was still missing from Minneapolis. . . .

Because all the women had been approached initially within the Hennepin County borders, Carver County investigators working on the attack on Gwen Burton contacted the Hennepin Sheriff's Office. Carver County detectives Thiede and Al Otterdahl came in to meet with Hennepin County detectives Captain Ostlund and Archie Sonenstahl on September 17, 1974.

Thiede and Otterdahl briefed the Hennepin County detectives on the progress they had made in the Burton investigation.

The description of the attacker—"forty-five to fifty, balding with a dome-shaped forehead, green work uniform"—rang a bell with Ostlund and Sonenstahl. When they heard the specifics of the sexual attack—particularly the use of a claw-hammer handle as a dildo—they remembered the Jerri Billings case. The man who had abducted Jerri had forced a hammer into her vagina too. It was a bizarre kind of sex attack, something that indicated a commonality, a similar M.O.

The car used to transport Gwen had been a four-door green Chevrolet Caprice—possibly a 1965 to 1968 model—with a black interior.

Archie Sonenstahl, a veteran homicide detective with the Hennepin County Sheriff's Office, was about to be plunged into the biggest case of his career. A blue-eyed Scandinavian in his late thirties, Sonenstahl could not know then how intricate the chase would become. The warning sent from Seattle had never reached him; it had long since disappeared under a ton of paperwork. He had never heard of Duane Homan or Billy Baughman. The Seattle detectives worked more than two thousand miles away. But the three men were destined to meet soon.

And Archie Sonenstahl would one day soon join the list of Harvey Carignan's least favorite people.

Sonenstahl accompanied Thiede and Otterdahl when they returned to the intensive-care unit of Abbott Hospital to interview Gwen Burton again. As he listened to Gwen describe her attacker, he saw more similarities to the man who had kidnapped Jerri Billings in September 1973. The clothing was similar, the language was similar; in some instances, the obscenities used were identical. Both girls had been threatened with a claw hammer, and both girls had been "raped" with its handle. Jerri had escaped the murderous bludgeoning that Gwen had endured. Otherwise, everything matched.

When Sonenstahl found the report made by the woman who had escaped her attacker only because she wore a wig, he toted up another case that matched the M.O. of the balding rapist.

Sonenstahl realized that there was a need for haste. Already the man had attacked Jerri, Gwen, and the wigged woman. Sonenstahl did not yet know about June Lynch and

Lisa King. Nor had he any reason at this time to include the disappearance of Eileen Hunley in the pattern.

He did know one thing, based upon his many years as a detective. The man he sought seemed obsessed, and would continue attacking Minnesota women until he was stopped.

12

Archie Sonenstahl barely had time to gird for the all-out search for the rapist in the green Chevrolet. The next day, when he arrived at the Criminal Division offices on Wednesday morning, September 18, he found an all-points bulletin on the teletype from the Sherburne County, Minnesota, Sheriff's Office.

Detectives in the Sherburne County office were attempting to establish the identity of a body found in that county—which lies north of the Minneapolis area. On September 17 Sherburne County officers had been summoned to a wooded area near Zimmerman, Minnesota, by a citizen who had stumbled upon the corpse. The only information on the teletype was that the body was that of a Caucasian female and that the corpse was badly decomposed.

Sonenstahl called the Sherburne detectives and asked for whatever additional specifics they might have.

"She's been dead awhile—the pathologist says a minimum of two weeks, and it could be more. The body's very decomposed. We're setting a tentative age of twenty-three years, but it could vary a few years either way."

"Do you have a cause of death?" Sonenstahl asked, and held his breath unconsciously.

"Bludgeon wounds to the skull—probably with a hammer."

Sonenstahl told the Sherburne County detective about the attack on Gwen Burton. "Our victim is alive, but critically injured. The man who attacked her used a claw hammer. She was picked up in Minneapolis and taken south, and it sounds like your body site is about twenty-five miles north of here, but—''

"Right. I can see the similarities."

"Was your victim sexually assaulted?" Sonenstahl asked.

"Yes . . . but not normally."

"What do you mean?"

"The body is so decomposed that most of the abdominal and genital tissue is desiccated. But . . . well . . . there was a tree branch—the killer had jammed it into the vagina."

"That fits with our case. Our victim was assaulted that way with a hammer."

"Keep us informed of your investigation?"

Sonenstahl promised that he would. But the case was looking worse instead of better; now it looked as if an actual murder might be attributed to the man he sought. He had certainly intended to kill Gwen Burton, perhaps thought that he had killed her when he left her comatose in the gully.

One of the things that bothered Sonenstahl most was the fact that the attacks were taking place so close together. With most serial rapists and murderers, there is a period of weeks or months between incidents. Now, September was barely half over, and it looked like the suspect had begun his siege in August with the murder of the woman found in Sherburne County and then continued to attack women within a few days of each preceding attack.

Sonenstahl contacted the Goodhue County Sheriff's Office in Red Wing and requested their assistance in finding the man that Jerri Billings had tentatively identified at the training school's church service eleven months before. Perhaps she had pointed out the right man, after all.

"If you find him," Sonenstahl added, "would you see if he owns a Chevrolet Caprice or if there is one available to him?"

Next he called Agent Tom Brownell of the Minnesota Bureau of Criminal Apprehension and asked that a driver's-license photo of the man—identified by the Goodhue County Sheriff's Office as Karl Olafson—be forwarded. Sonenstahl would incorporate it into a "lay-down"—a montage of mug shots to be shown to the victims.

Since some of the girls had been abducted within the Minneapolis city limits, Sonenstahl called the Minneapolis Police Department and asked for an assist from that department. Detective Doug Nordmeyer was assigned to the investigation.

The next abduction reported occurred on Wednesday, September 18. The Minneapolis Police Department received a complaint on Thursday, the nineteenth, from Sally Versoi, eighteen.

The complaint was transferred to Doug Nordmeyer's desk. Sally Versoi described an incident that would become chillingly familiar.

"I was hitchhiking at eight-thirty in the morning yesterday when a man driving a light green 1971 Chevrolet Caprice stopped to pick me up. He was about fifty, maybe six feet, two inches tall, about two-hundred pounds, and he wore green work pants. . . ."

Sally said that the man had offered her twenty-five dollars if she would go with him to the country north of Minneapolis to pick up a car and drive it back for him. She had been on her way to school at the Work Opportunity Center when she was picked up.

Intrigued by the offer of that much money, she had told the man that she would go with him but that she had to stop at the school first to meet a girlfriend: Diane Flynn, seventeen.

The man promised that he would take her to the school and then come back and pick them up a little after nine A.M. He did come back and the trio left, heading north.

"He talked to us along the way," Sally said. "I remember he told us this story about him being robbed and beaten on the head with a hammer. This sounded familiar to me. You see, one of the girls at the Work Opportunity Center was attacked and beaten with a hammer earlier this month. I knew she was hurt so bad that she ended up in the hospital."

But Sally hadn't been frightened at that point, and she hadn't known the details of how the girl at school had met her attacker. If she had, she never would have agreed to go with the man in the green Chevy.

Both Sally and Diane thought that the man was a bit

strange, but they assumed they would be all right because there were two of them.

The man at the wheel drove at one point into a deserted area, and the girls looked around but couldn't see another car. He stopped and turned toward them, and asked a question that they doubted he'd asked for purely philosophical reasons.

"If you had a choice, would you rather be raped or killed?"

Both girls responded instantly, "We'd rather be killed."

The man grunted, and started to drive again.

Diane was sitting in the middle of the front seat, and Sally was next to the door. Diane was wary and suspicious, and she said something to the driver that he found irritating.

"When are we going to get there?" she complained. "If it's much farther, this won't be worth the money."

The driver snapped his right hand from the wheel and backhanded Diane in the face—hard. Diane's mouth started to bleed from a cut lip, and two of her teeth were chipped.

"Hey," Sally intervened. "None of that. Stop and let us change places. I'll sit in the middle and Diane can sit by the door."

She was hoping that when they stopped, she and Diane would be able to get away from the guy, but he stopped only long enough for them to change places. He stood beside the car, and there was no chance for them to run.

She was praying, and planning how to escape, when the man breathed an oath, and she saw that he was staring at his gas gauge, where the indicator was pointing to "Empty."

When they stopped at a gas station in St. Francis, she and Diane were able to get out of the car and run into the station.

They reported the strange encounter as soon as they could find a way back to Minneapolis.

Both girls were certain that the big man intended to either rape or kill them, but he'd apparently changed his mind for some reason.

"Now, I think he was probably the same guy that took a hammer to the girl from school. . . ."

Sonenstahl had hoped that the suspect originally fingered by Jerri Billings was going to look good for all of it, but he had a disappointment when the Goodhue County Sheriff's Office reported back on Karl Olafson.

"We checked him out. He couldn't be your man. He has no access to a green Caprice—nobody's ever seen him driving one—and, more than that, we checked his work schedule and he was definitely working when the attacks occurred. Straight family man. No record."

Evidently Karl Olafson had been a look-alike for the real suspect, and that was all.

He was, indeed, a look-alike. On September 20 Sally Versoi and Dianne Flynn came into the Minneapolis police offices to talk with Nordmeyer and Sonenstahl. Their description of their abductor's language matched the earlier recollection of Gwen Burton. They recalled that he smoked constantly—regular-size Camels. They remembered his sideburns, scruffy-looking unshaven areas that extended almost to his chin. They spoke of the pronounced furrows that grooved his cheeks, and a deep dimple in his chin.

Shown a lay-down of twelve photos, both girls chose the third picture in the series. "That looks a lot like him—but it isn't him."

The picture was of Karl Olafson—already eliminated from consideration in the probe because he had been at work. The best the detectives could say was they had a picture of a man who *looked* like the man they sought.

Better than nothing, but not much better.

Next Nordmeyer and Sonenstahl went to see the principal of the Work Opportunity Center. It looked like two pairs of girls from the same school had fallen victim to the man who preyed on teenage hitchhikers. For some reason, the Minneapolis-based detectives had not received a copy of the case file involving June Lynch and Lisa King.

"Yes," the principal responded to their questions about an earlier attack, "two of our girls were involved in an attack on September 8. I can give you June Lynch's home address. Let's see . . . she lives on Colfax Avenue South."

The detective team located June Lynch in the foster home where she lived and found that she had been struck with a hammer and suffered severe injuries earlier in the month. She repeated the statement that she'd given just after the incident to Kanabec County deputies. And the details were, of course, very similar to the other attacks.

Now there were six, possibly seven young women who had encountered the man the detectives sought. June looked at the twelve photos in the montage, and she too pointed to number three.

"It's not him—but it looks like him."

Of course. But who was he?

Due to the similarities of all the cases that had emerged so far, Archie Sonenstahl scheduled a meeting for September 23 in the Hennepin County Courthouse in Minneapolis. Detectives from Hennepin, Carver, Sherburne, and Kanabec counties and from the Minneapolis Police Department said that they would attend, along with members of the Minnesota State Bureau of Criminal Apprehension, and pathologist Dr. Calvin Bandt of the Hennepin County Medical Examiner's Office.

But even as they planned the meeting that would allow them to share information, the suspect had struck again.

Kathy Schultz, eighteen, lived with her family on Pleasant Avenue South in Minneapolis. Like four of the other victims, Kathy attended the Work Opportunity School in the evenings to learn keypunch operation, and during the daytime hours she went to Washburn High School. Like Kathy Miller, Kathy Schultz was a pretty girl with long blond hair, parted in the middle and falling down her back. And, like the other Kathy, she was a young woman whose loving personality lit up the world around her.

Kathy Schultz was a free spirit, a teenager especially gifted with kindness and sensitivity to other people's problems. She was a good listener, and willingly shared her friends' burdens. But she herself was happy, a girl who often proclaimed that she loved life.

Paradoxically, as much as Kathy Schultz loved life, she seemed somehow to know that she would not live to be an old woman. She spoke of it to friends, not with the somber words of a doomsayer, but with a conviction that she had to taste as much of life as she could because she would not have endless years to do so.

Kathy wrote poetry that, in retrospect, shivers the spine.

When I go away, maybe today or tomorrow
I'll just fly away—
So I won't have to say
So long . . .

And another poem which she wrote music for, and played on her guitar:

Put a white rose on my grave,
And talk to me of good times.
Don't cry, but be brave,
For we only have one lifetime . . .

Put a white rose on my grave
And talk to me of good times.
Think of all the love we gave
And our lovely walks in springtime.

Why would such a healthy, pretty young woman be so preoccupied with her own early death? Perhaps she sensed something that no one who loved her could have predicted.

And still, despite the specter of death that walked with her, Kathy Schultz planned for her future. She loved the woods and fields of flowers so much that she said she wanted to study forestry. "Then I could live much of my life outdoors."

Although Kathy wasn't sure if she would work or go to college after high school, she felt that she had found herself and that she was in control of her own life. The youngest in a family of four children, she came after two sisters, twenty-five and twenty-one, and a brother of twenty-three.

She was much loved.

Things had been perfectly normal in the Schultz household on Friday morning—September 20. Kathy's brother, Steven, was the last to see her. That was at 7:45 A.M., and Kathy was in her pajamas, picking out clothes to wear when she stopped by the Work Opportunity School on an errand. Kathy was in a good mood as her brother called good-bye to her and left, leaving her alone in the house. Ordinarily Kathy would have left the house about eight and have been home from school when her family returned in the late afternoon.

When dusk fell on September 20, Kathy's family began to grow frantic with worry over her. They checked with Kathy's friends, but no one had seen her. Like Mary Miller had done two years and five months before, they sat up all night waiting for Kathy to come home or call.

She did not.

Her mother checked her room and saw the last thing Kathy had written, some paragraphs scribbled on a sheet of paper. It was not a poem, it was an essay telling the world how much life meant to her. It began: "If I should die . . ."

Mrs. Shultz had no way of determining what Kathy had been wearing that day; she had so many clothes. But Kathy always wore a bright red bandanna, and that was gone. That would help when she called the police and asked them to look for Kathy. The distinctive bright red bandanna.

And yet she could not shake the memory of Kathy's "If I should die . . ."

On Saturday, September 21, two pheasant hunters crept through fields of tall grass and corn shocks in Isanti County, some forty miles north of Minneapolis. The closest inhabited area was the small town of Dalbo, Minnesota. Looking for a flash of tailfeathers, listening for the rustle of wings lifted in alarm, the hunters were shocked into silence at what they found in the field.

"Oh, my God," one of them finally breathed. "Oh, my God."

The body of a slender woman lay crumpled among the tall corn shocks. They could not see her face; her head had been destroyed by a rain of crushing blows, and her long hair was stained crimson with her own blood.

Something paler red fluttered in the breeze. It was a red bandanna, still tied around her neck.

The hunters forgot about pheasants and raced to their truck to call Isanti County deputies.

The toll was now eight.

13

The meeting of all involved police agencies that Archie Sonenstahl had set for Monday morning, September 23, was held on schedule. But now there was another agency on the roster: Isanti County.

Detective Frisk of the Hennepin County Sheriff's Office had been notified of the newest body find on Saturday by the Isanti detectives. "Initial pathology reports indicate that the victim was sexually assaulted and succumbed to severe head injuries, probably caused by a 'hammerlike' object."

Now Isanti detectives—along with spokesmen from all other jurisdictions where women had been found dead, or where they had been attacked—presented their cases. After the exchange of information, there could be no question that they were all looking for the same man. The man who had driven a blue pickup truck with a silver camper in 1973 and who now drove a pale green Chevrolet Caprice with a black interior. The man with the hammer.

Victims' descriptions had varied little. Some of the girls had pegged their attacker to be six-foot-one, some six-two or six-three. That was an understandable variance; historically, witnesses are off on height more than any other estimate.

But all the young women had described a man with a dome-shaped forehead, balding with grayish-brown hair, long sideburns, deeply lined cheeks, and a dimple in his chin. He always wore green work clothes, the pants rolled or tucked into heavy work boots, which indicated his occupation involved some kind of manual labor. He smoked Camels, and his language was crude and obscene. And he was strong—terribly strong—a powerful man who hadn't been at all nervous about taking on two girls at once.

Sonenstahl listed the clues they had on a chalk board. He distributed pictures of Karl Olafson, the man who resembled the suspect they sought. "This isn't the man, but he looks like the man. Keep this to yourselves."

The Chevrolet Caprice was probably the most valuable clue they had. Since the killer apparently moved freely, unaware that detectives knew so much about him, he probably was still driving that car.

The detectives tried to figure out what kind of sex monster they were dealing with. It was quite possible that the "rapist" was impotent. The girls who had survived had been forced to commit oral sodomy. But actual vaginal penetration had not occurred. Instead, the suspect had used a claw-hammer handle as a substitute. It was possible that the killer was unable to achieve an erection, that rage over his own impotence made him seek artificial and sadistic ways to satisfy his sexual drives. To the layman, this might seem unusual. To the experienced detectives present, this wasn't news. They had seen impotent "rapists" before.

"We think our crimes are interrelated," Sonenstahl summarized. "I suggest that we consider this a joint investigation, with all jurisdictions cooperating."

It was agreed by all present at that early Monday morning meeting. The joint case number would henceforth be 204.

Although the probers had living witnesses, physical evidence was a problem. The skulls of the women who had died were so shattered that there were no definitive weapon marks to compare with the murder weapon if the detectives should locate possibles. As in the cases of Kathy Miller and Laura Leslie Brock, the skull damage had been inflicted on the left side of the head, indicating that the killer was right-handed.

The killer had already demonstrated that he knew how to make it difficult for detectives; he had taken each victim (or set of victims) into a different county to act out his sadism. He had bought time by doing this, time he had now run out of. . . .

Deputy Sheriff Edgar Olson of Isanti County announced that his county *did* have some physical evidence. "We have a plaster cast of a tire tread found at the site of Kathy Schultz's body. We've had it examined by local tire wholesalers and they believe it's an Atlas brand, belted tire."

Olson turned the cast over to Sonenstahl for comparison with the tires on the Chevrolet Caprice—if it were ever found.

All the detectives attending the meeting in the Hennepin County Courthouse agreed that the killer probably lived in Minneapolis, and probably in the southern part of the city—close to the Work Opportunity Center. If they got lucky, the green Chevy might be spotted in the area.

Archie Sonenstahl compiled a confidential memo describing everything that was known about the Caprice, and included a description of the suspect; it was issued to all patrolmen in police agencies within a hundred miles of Minneapolis: "Hennepin County Sheriff's Office requests that such a vehicle or individual be observed and identification of same obtained."

At the time of the joint meeting on September 23, the nameless body still lay unidentified in the morgue in Sherburne County. With no personal effects, it was almost impossible to identify this decomposed corpse. At first considered to be in her early twenties by pathologists, this body seemed not to be part of the pattern established by the rapist-killer—the pattern that dictated he abduct and attack young women in their teens. No one knew at this time that the dead woman found in Sherburne County was actually close to thirty. No one knew that she had been the latest beloved of Harvey Carignan.

But then, none of the detectives had heard of Harvey Carignan, either.

That lack was remedied on September 24. If there is justice in the justice system, the balance finally shifted on that Tuesday in Minneapolis. This time, the police had the luck.

Two Minneapolis police patrolmen, working in the south sector of the city, observed a big bald man wearing green work clothes and boots. They watched as he headed across a parking lot, and they waited to see which vehicle he would approach. They doubted that he would be the man they sought; they'd only just received the bulletin, and things in police work were seldom so quickly accomplished.

However, the tall man stopped beside a 1968 pale green Chevrolet Caprice!

The officers pulled in behind the Chevy as it exited the parking lot, and the driver picked up speed and attempted to lose them, darting in and out of traffic, turning onto side streets. The officers stayed right behind the car, and put on their whirling blue lights to signal the driver to stop. Stymied in his evasive actions, the big man behind the wheel pulled over.

When the officers approached the Chevrolet, they saw that it did indeed have a black interior. The driver identified himself as Harvey Louis Carignan and gave an address in the 2600 block of 13th Avenue South in Minneapolis. The officers noted that he had begun to sweat profusely and that his right eye and forehead were twitching with nervousness.

"You are under arrest, sir," the officer stated. "We're taking you down to headquarters for questioning on murder charges. You have the right to remain silent. You have the right to an attorney—"

Harvey waved his hand. "I know all that shit."

Lieutenant Searles of the Minneapolis Police Department and Detective Archie Sonenstahl looked at the man seated in the interview room. He was almost a dead ringer for Karl Olafson, the original suspect—but not quite. He was bigger and more muscular, and he was nervous as hell. Sonenstahl read Carignan his rights under Miranda again, and Carignan nodded.

He was quite willing to discuss the charges. He proclaimed his innocence, and appeared to feel that he could convince the detectives that it was all a mistake.

The suspect took on a pious expression and explained that he believed in the teachings of the church, "especially the two commandments 'Love thy Lord' and 'Love thy neighbor.' "

Harvey stated that one must repent his sins, but he declined to elaborate on that thought. No, he himself had no sins that he felt compelled to repent; he had made the statement more for the detectives' benefit.

In answer to less philosophical questions, he replied that, yes, of course he had helped the girl whose car was stalled in the Sears lot. He remembered her well; she'd had short brown hair and was wearing slacks or jeans. "I looked at her car and told her I couldn't fix it without my tools, so I just gave her a ride across the lot and dropped her off in front of the Sears entrance."

No, he hadn't taken her into Carver County. Of course not.

"Do you carry a blue plaid blanket in your car?" Sonenstahl asked.

"Yes. There's no law against that, is there?"

"Could I see your wallet?" Sonenstahl asked, and Harvey handed it over.

The Hennepin County detective was interested to find a sales slip for tires purchased on August 12, 1974, in Belvidere, Illinois. The tires were Atlas G78-14. These would be very close to the plaster cast that Isanti County detectives had retrieved from the field where Kathy Schultz's body was dumped. Sonenstahl handed the wallet back without commenting.

Next Harvey was queried about the incident involving the girls from the Work Opportunity School on September 18.

"Do you remember picking up two girls last week and driving them out in the boonies and having an argument—and leaving them there?"

Without thinking through it, Harvey blurted, "I never, never got into an argument with any girls, and I've never been to Mora. I never hit any girl."

Sonenstahl felt a rush. He had not mentioned Mora, and he hadn't said anything about striking a girl. Harvey was telling too much, and he was getting his girls mixed up.

Smoothly Sonenstahl let it pass, and switched gears. "Harvey, do you remember picking up a hitchhiker—a young woman—last Friday? That would have been . . . let's see . . . on the twentieth."

"I think I do remember picking up a gal on Fifty-fourth or

Fifty-sixth and Lyndale sometime in the morning on Friday. She was on her way to that school on Colfax and Lake Street. She had on a red bandanna.''

Sonenstahl kept his voice calm, but he felt elation inside. ''Where did you let her off?''

''I let her off at Lyndale and Lake.''

''You're sure? You're sure you didn't take her for a drive out in the country?''

''No, sir. I just took her to the corner of Lyndale and Lake. She wasn't really a girl, either; she was in her early twenties.''

''She was eighteen,'' Sonenstahl said quietly.

Harvey shrugged.

The spot where Harvey said he picked up the hitchhiker in the red bandanna was three blocks from Kathy Schultz's home.

Harvey's response to questioning was interesting. He denied any culpability in the attacks on the victims, but he told just enough to place the girls in his company on the vital days, apparently thinking that if he told half the story, it would make him appear innocent.

And he was clever, too; he had good reason to suspect that some of the victims might have left fingerprints in his car. If he said he had never seen them at all, how could he explain their fingerprints in his Chevy? He was clearly attempting to cover all bases.

Sonenstahl knew in his gut that he had the right man, but he suspended the interrogation for the time being and returned Harvey to his cell in the Hennepin County Jail. He needed some verification from his eyewitnesses.

By eleven A.M. Sonenstahl had arranged for a lineup which included Harvey Carignan, along with several other men who matched his same general description. Viewing the lineup through one-way glass were Lisa King, June Lynch, Diane Flynn, and Sally Versoi. Each girl was given a form showing stick figures with numbers on them.

''Study the men you see on the platform,'' Sonenstahl instructed. ''If you see the man who attacked you, put an X on the number that corresponds to the man's position on the platform.''

The four girls watched as the men faced forward, to the

left, to the right, and then each of them marked the position occupied by Harvey Carignan. None of them had any doubt at all.

Twelve photos were incorporated into a new "lay-down" and taken to Abbott Hospital, where Gwen Burton remained in the intensive-care unit. Gwen looked at them, and gasped when she saw Harvey's mug shot.

"That's him. I don't want to look at it anymore."

Now detectives fanned out and questioned every acquaintance of Harvey Carignan's they could find. This prong of the investigation elicited the information that Harvey had had a girlfriend, Eileen Marie Hunley, whose birthdate was July 17, 1945.

"Only Eileen's gone," an informant said. "Nobody's seen her since August 10."

A search warrant was obtained for Eileen's apartment at 1408 Spruce Street. No blood was found, nothing to indicate that a struggle had taken place in the apartment itself, but the detectives did find a bill addressed to Miss Hunley from a dentist in Kansas City. The dentist's name and address were relayed at once to the Hennepin County Medical Examiner's Office.

"If you can get the charts from him," Sonenstahl suggested, "you may be able to identify the body found up in Sherburne County."

When the charts and teeth were compared, Dr. Bandt saw that the alignment and dental work were identical: the body was that of Eileen Hunley.

On September 24 and 25, search warrants were obtained for the room Harvey rented and for his vehicle. Probable cause to believe that he was involved in these specific crimes against women had been carefully established by the task force and listed to obtain the warrants. Sonenstahl and his crew of detectives were taking no chances at all that their suspect would find a loophole in the law.

The room and the Chevrolet were remarkably clean. But the Chevy's new Atlas tires proved to be exactly the size and configuration as the tires that had left the tread marks in the field next to Kathy Schultz's body.

Sonenstahl checked with the Minnesota Motor Vehicles Department and found that Harvey had purchased the 1968 Caprice eight months before, on January 6, 1974, after trading off his previous vehicle, a 1968 Chevrolet pickup similar to the one that Jerri Billings described in her statement about the attack in September 1973. Jerri had thought that the truck that picked her up was a pale color with a metallic camper on top.

The Minnesota detectives contacted the registered owner, who lived in North Minneapolis.

The new owner led the investigators to a shed where the pickup was stored. "I only drove it a hundred and thirty miles, and it's been stored ever since," he explained.

That might be a real bonus; if the pickup had been used so little since Harvey turned it over, there might still be evidence inside that would help.

The truck was neither yellow and black nor a pale color; the new owner had removed all the paint down to the prime coat, and it was impossible to determine what color it had once been. The owner said it had been bright yellow and black before he took the paint off, but he couldn't remember which, if any, earlier coats of paint had been underneath the garish colors.

If there was some question about the color of the newly discovered truck, there was no question at all in Jerri Billings' mind when she was led into the lineup room and watched a half-dozen men parade across the stage. Like all the other girls, she pointed to Harvey Carignan. "That's the man—that's the one who picked me up last year."

Detectives Sonenstahl and Merrill drove Jerri to the garage where Harvey's previous vehicle was still stored, and asked her to look it over. She nodded her head as she pointed out identifying parts on the exterior of the truck, and then she looked inside and said that the bucket seats were the same, as was the board between the seats. She was sure that the pickup was the same truck in which she'd taken her ride of terror thirteen months before.

With the new owner's permission, Sonenstahl checked the

area beneath the front seat. There he could see and feel several folded maps, and a quantity of long hair. . . .

The pickup was towed into the police garage for processing. During the hours-long processing, Sonenstahl and lab technicians retrieved the number of strands of human hair, believed to be female in origin. The hairs were not all from the same person, but represented a variety of colors. Each sample was bagged, sealed, and initialed and sent to the lab for isolation as to class and characteristics under a scanning electron microscope. While human hair is not absolute physical evidence and cannot be positively traced back to one human source, it is regarded to be highly probable physical evidence. When a number of hairs are found from many different sources, and found to be alike in class and characteristics with different victims' hair, the probability factor takes a quantum leap.

If, for instance, even three victims' probable hair should be found in a suspect's car, the chance that the hair is not theirs is one in 20,000, according to Bob Neill, for two decades an FBI expert on hair-and-fiber analysis.

Beyond the hairs found in Harvey's former vehicle—the pickup he left Seattle in—Sonenstahl studied the road maps. Maps from Washington, Oregon, Idaho, California, Montana, Wisconsin, and Kansas.

It was not unusual for a man who traveled as much as Harvey did to have maps in his vehicles. What piqued Archie Sonenstahl's interest were markings on the maps—Harvey had placed 181 red circles around seemingly isolated areas. *Why?*

Archie Sonenstahl had obtained Harvey Carignan's rap sheet, and he saw that although his suspect had been in a lot of trouble in Minnesota in the sixties, he was clean in the recent past. He also saw that Harvey had apparently moved his operations in the mid-sixties to Seattle. Sonenstahl contacted Seattle detectives and found that he and detectives Duane Homan and Billy Baughman had a lot in common.

Baughman and Homan were not surprised to hear that Harvey was under arrest in Minneapolis; they were only surprised that it hadn't happened sooner. When they learned that two women had died and several others had barely escaped with their lives, they felt sick. If only they could have stopped him before . . .

But they had tried every way they could and still remain within the tight parameters of the law. And all they had been able to come up with had been the third-degree-assault charge filed by Alice Carignan, and that had been dropped as soon as Harvey turned on the tears and the charm with his estranged wife.

This case represented one of the ironies of police work; it wasn't the first in which they'd been sure they had a killer almost within their grasp, and then had had to watch him walk away blithely for lack of physical evidence. But, still, it was agonizing to know that this man had been connected with the violent murders of women and girls for *twenty-five* years and had never been convicted of that worst of all crimes.

There had been Minnesota maps found when Baughman and Homan had issued their search warrant on Alice Carignan's home in north Seattle. Those maps had had red circles too, but they seemed innocuous at the time. Alice had told the detective pair that Harvey was having a difficult time finding work in Minnesota, and they assumed that the circles marked places where he'd applied for jobs. There were so many circles on the Minnesota map that when Homan described them to Sonenstahl, it seemed that their original supposition had been correct.

"We couldn't have had that many attacks here—all unreported," the Hennepin County detective replied. "Maybe one or two, but certainly not that many."

Communications between Seattle and Minneapolis flew thick and fast now. Homan and Baughman forwarded all information on the Kathy Miller case and their subsequent protracted investigation, as did Undersheriff Bob Sharp of Island County with his unsolved murder of Laura Leslie Brock.

The circle around Coupeville, Washington, probably *did* indicate a "kill" in the Island County area. The last sighting of Laura Brock had her getting into a pickup truck with a white or silver canopy top—the truck located by Sonenstahl in north Minneapolis? The canopy top was still silver. Perhaps even more telling, the pickup had been modified by the addition of a second gas tank. The filler pipe for this second tank stuck out from the side of the truck. Was this the pipe jutting out of the side of the pickup that witnesses had described after they saw Laura Brock accept a ride?

In Yakima County, Washington, deputies began the almost impossible task of digging up isolated regions where red circles had appeared. A possible grave site near the Hell's Crossing campground on the American River seemed the most likely. A deer hunter had spied a three-by-four-foot square of dirt that had sunk into the ground, as if it had been dug up and refilled.

But there was nothing—or no one—in that strange hole. There were eight more circles on the Yakima County portion of the map. Other locations marked in Washington state included Ross Lake, Diablo Dam, Ross Dam, the Cowlitz River, the Snoqualmie National Forest, Hogback Mountain, and Greenwater. If a body had been secreted in any of those places, it would have returned to earth long ago.

The awful possibility remained that there were innumerable bodies of women who had been murdered within those circled areas. Harvey's first wife had told of his obsession with keeping records, either in his head or scribbled on paper. Were these maps circled with scarlet a record of death?

It might be impossible to be sure—ever.

And Kathy Miller? There was a circle around the Tulalip Indian Reservation, the lonely region where Kathy's body had been found.

Maps outside of Washington might also have coded markings of possible body sites. There was a small map of Medora, North Dakota, in the pickup truck, with circles and symbols drawn on it. Sonenstahl called law-enforcement authorities there and found that a fourteen-year-old girl had been found murdered less than two miles west of Medora on April 30, 1973, her body found only two days before Kathy Miller was seized. It had lain undiscovered for some time.

Sonenstahl received a communication from the Johnson County Sheriff's Office in Olathe, Kansas. They too had an unidentified female homicide victim, found on June 19, 1974.

Investigation revealed that Harvey and Eileen Hunley had visited Miss Hunley's home in Goessel, Kansas, on the previous weekend. Eileen's home was less than eighty miles from the body site in Johnson County. Eileen's family remembered that Harvey had left their home occasionally during that weekend, to be gone for several hours each time.

There were circles around two locations in Vancouver, British Columbia—one of Harvey's favorite travel spots—one marked Exhibition Park and the other West 67th Avenue and Oak Street. Canadian detectives had an open case in Vancouver that matched Harvey's alleged M.O. A young woman waiting for a bus had been attacked by a man who beat her with a claw hammer. She had been waiting at a bus stop on West 67th and Oak Street. . . .

Harvey Carignan's arrest made headlines in Seattle papers, as it did in Minnesota papers.

The photographs that accompanied the articles on his newest encounter with police authorities showed a gaunt man, a man who appeared to have lost twenty or thirty pounds since he'd fled Seattle to avoid Homan's and Baughman's questioning. The lines running on each side of his nose to his mouth had deepened, and his eyes stared blankly into the camera.

As the probe into his suspected crimes continued in Minnesota and across the Midwest, Harvey stayed in jail. Jailers found him quite amenable. One jailer described him as "a model prisoner—a gentleman, in fact."

14

Detectives throughout the northern states from Minnesota to Washington worked during the last few months of 1974 hunting for bodies, trying to correlate red circles to specific locations. And it proved to be an impossible task; there was simply too much space involved to find something as relatively small as a human body moldering in the earth—if, indeed, such bodies existed.

Nor could detectives in Johnson County, Kansas, and Medora, North Dakota, find evidence that might link Harvey Carignan inextricably to their cases. Nothing now beyond coincidence.

In Minnesota, Sonenstahl's task force was faring better: they had their tire-tread match and their eyewitnesses. But they did not have positive hair or fiber identification; the hairs beneath the seat of the pickup could not be traced back to known victims. Where the women are who left so many strands of their hair behind will never be known.

Nevertheless, there was enough evidence to bind Harvey Carignan over for trial, or, more precisely, for what promised to be a series of trials.

The case involving Gwen Burton, who had been taken to the lonely alfalfa field south of Minneapolis, sodomized, beaten, choked, and left for dead, would be first. District Judge Arlo Haering's Carver County courtroom in Chaska, Minnesota, was packed in the second week of February 1975 as potential jurors were questioned by Prosecutor William

Glaeser and defense attorneys Douglas Thomson and Joseph Friedberg.

By Friday, February 14, eight men and four women had been chosen as the primary jurors in the attempted-murder and aggravated-sodomy trial. Two alternate jurors would be chosen on the following Tuesday and the trial would begin. Through their rights of discovery, the defense team had requested and received all of the prosecution's "paper" (the police follow-ups, the witnesses' statements, the lab reports—everything), but the street did not run both ways. What Thomson and Freidberg would come up with as a defense plan for Harvey was a mystery. Few defense attorneys relish the prospect of dealing with a living eyewitness in an attempted-murder case, and Thomson and Freidberg had seen Gwen Burton's name on the state's witness list. Bets were on among detectives about what strategy Harvey's attorneys would employ.

Thomson hinted at what his defense would be when he told prospective jurors that the defense would not dispute that Harvey Carignan had "perpetrated the acts" he had been charged with, but he indicated that the mental state of his client at the time of the acts would be a key issue.

Not guilty by reason of insanity. It is a defense filled with pitfalls. One misstep and the defendant may find himself up to his neck in rhetorical quicksand.

In an insanity plea the defense attorneys must show that their client did not know the difference between right and wrong at the exact moment of murder. And who can say what was in another man's mind at one specific time?

Harvey Carignan had certainly taken pains to cover his tracks *after* his alleged crimes. He had destroyed a plethora of evidence, and he had thus far denied vociferously that he had harmed any woman. He had even made up his own carefully laundered versions of meeting the victims. Could a man legally insane have managed all of that?

Douglas Thomson was a well-known, highly respected attorney in the Midwest, and the prosecution waited to see what rabbits he would pull out of his hat. Thomson was hinting that Harvey might confess on the stand.

While speaking obliquely to the media before trial, Thomson would only say casually, "It is not an overly complicated case, so it should not be a protracted trial."

On Wednesday, February 19, 1975, Thomson rose to make his opening statement.

And then the fireworks began. Thomson had decided to beat the state to the punch; he laid out horror upon horror. He promised—or warned—jurors that the testimony they would hear would be "the most harrowing story you've ever heard."

Thomson and his co-attorney, Freidberg, admitted that Harvey Carignan's actions had been even more sordid than what had been charged by the prosecution. The defense promised to show that their client had been so "sexually traumatized" from infancy that he was schizophrenic—psychotic—by the time he reached his early twenties. They maintained that Harvey hated all women and that he truly considered it his divine mission to kill "the harlots and the whores."

"Harvey Carignan believes to this day as he sits here before you that he has failed the Lord," Friedberg stated. "He deliberately attempted to kill that young lady and he blames where he is right now on the fact that a woman would not die. If he could, he would go back now and finish it."

It was a bold, even dangerous approach. Harvey's own attorneys were stating that he was a monster, but a completely insane monster who should be committed, not to prison, but to a mental institution.

A mental institution was not what the prosecution had in mind at all; the State wanted Harvey safely behind bars in a maximum-security prison.

Friedberg said that the defense would describe Harvey's life from the time he was a child in North Dakota to the present. "We will show that at each and every juncture of his life he was sexually traumatized. In incident after incident, he was degraded—always by a woman."

Friedberg maintained that the incidents had begun when his client was only three or four years old and involved babysitters, Harvey's own mother, and a reformatory matron.

"We admit every fact," Friedberg continued. "It is possible we will show you that the act was more sordid and more fiendish than the prosecutor says.''

Friedberg asserted that even Gwen Burton might not remember how bad it had been, that she might have blocked memories that were too horrific to remember. If she did not remember and therefore could not relate her recollections accurately to the prosecutor and the detectives, then, Friedberg hinted, the defense might know more about the crime than the state.

The defense attorneys' knowledge of the crimes had, of course, come straight from the lips of Harvey Carignan. To those of a suspicious bent, the question of Harvey's ''editing'' arose. But apparently Harvey had shown his lawyers a crazy, sadistic side to his personality that had made the hairs prickle beneath their starched white shirt collars.

Rather than let Glaeser bring out all the ugly details, what Thomson and Friedberg had done, in essence, was to defuse the thrust of Prosecutor Glaeser's case. When Glaeser began to present his witnesses, the defense could say, ''Well, look at this. We've already told you how bad it was, and we're going to show you that it all happened because our client is totally insane.''

The jury looked at the defendant. Harvey Carignan sat stolidly, as he would throughout the trial, staring at the floor, or at his huge hands, or at the wall. His lined face drooped. He looked . . . what? Mad? Insane? Perhaps only sullen and slightly superior. He was good at looking aloof and superior; he had practiced that air since childhood.

The prosecution had a small ace of its own up the sleeve. Harvey had told Archie Sonenstahl of his hatred for Duane Homan and Billy Baughman, and the Minnesota detective perceived that there was more than hatred there: there was fear. It seemed that if any man might break through Harvey's ''crazy'' act, it would be either Homán or Baughman. Harvey seemed to feel that the Seattle detectives had always been able to read his thoughts and that they would continue to dog him all his life.

Sonenstahl had called Duane Homan before the trial and invited him to attend. ''It might be interesting if you flew here and simply sat in the courtroom. He hates your guts—but it's more than that; he's afraid of you.''

"I'm not real comfortable around him either." Homan laughed. "If I come there, Archie, you've got to promise that I get a seat on the aisle. I've seen Harvey when he was angry, and I don't want anybody sitting between me and the door if he flips out. Promise?''

"I guarantee you can pick any seat in the courtroom," Sonenstahl said. "Duane, we think he's going to confess everything once he gets up on the stand. Your cases. Our cases. *Everything*. I think you'll want to be here when he tells it all to the jury.''

"You bet I do," Homan responded.

And so Duane Homan booked a flight to Minneapolis, and left the rain of Seattle behind for the bitter cold of a Minnesota winter.

Duane Homan's face was unfamiliar to everyone in the courthouse in Chaska, Minnesota—everyone except Harvey Carignan. He was not deliberately disguising his identity as he waited outside the courtroom for trial to begin; neither did he introduce himself to the defense team. He stood quietly by as one of the defense lawyers talked to Archie Sonenstahl. He heard the lawyer tell Sonenstahl that Harvey had admitted to his attorneys that he had killed both Laura Leslie Brock and Kathy Sue Miller in Washington.

When Sonenstahl nodded toward Homan and identified him to the defense team, their faces betrayed shock. They had not meant for Homan to hear about their client's admissions concerning the Washington crimes. But he *had* overheard. What he might be able to do with that long-awaited information was another matter; the confession had been made in a privileged-information situation, and there was still no physical evidence. Homan hoped that Harvey would confess to Kathy's and Laura's murders in open court.

Duane Homan walked through the courtroom doors and sat in the front row, close behind the man he had sought to arrest for so long. He stared at the back of Harvey's head and watched the powerful shoulders flex as Harvey shifted from time to time in his chair.

But Harvey never looked around. If he knew Homan was sitting behind him, he did not indicate it.

Carver County Prosecutor William Glaeser, undeterred by the defense head start, went through the facts of the case, recreating the stark horror of that day in September when Gwen Burton had encountered Harvey Carignan.

He told of how Gwen had been ordered into Harvey's car and then been driven out to the country where no one would hear her scream. He told of how Carignan had told Gwen, "Come over and sit by me."

"He then grabbed her by the hair and jerked her toward him. She resisted but then became fearful and decided that for her own safety she had better go along with what he wanted."

Women in the courtroom paled as Glaeser described the three instances of oral sodomy, the choking, the beating, and Harvey's sly answer when Gwen asked if he was going to kill her. "You shouldn't say things like that, you'll give me ideas."

He described Gwen's agonized crawl through the fields to find help, and her final rescue by the boy on the tractor.

Detective Al Otterdahl from Carver County testified to Gwen's statements to him as she lay in the intensive-care unit, and Archie Sonenstahl described his conversations with Gwen, and, subsequently, with Harvey. There was a ripple in the courtroom when Sonenstahl repeated Harvey's avowed belief in the commandments "Love thy Lord" and "Love thy neighbor."

Rumor had it that both Gwen Burton and Harvey Carignan would testify, and each morning found lines of spectators prepared to fight for a place in the courtroom.

Could a young woman who had suffered as Gwen Burton had find the courage to testify in front of a man who—according to his own attorneys—would still delight in killing her if he was given the opportunity? Would she feel safe, even now, with only a stretch of courtroom between them—despite the presence of armed deputies?

When the day in court was over, Duane Homan visited the county jail. He was led back through the cellblock to the high-security cell where Harvey was housed. It was actually a cell within a cell. Harvey's immediate cell was enclosed by another cell, like a child's steel box puzzle. If he should by the wildest stretch of the imagination get out of the inner cell, he would not be able to break through the surrounding bars.

Homan stopped and attempted to get Harvey to look at him, but the huge man would not meet his eyes. And then Harvey turned his head slowly and looked directly at the Seattle detective, and smiled faintly. He reached one arm up, and then the other, and his biceps bulged as he grasped the bars of the outer cell above him. He chinned himself, his massive body moving gracefully and easily up and down.

"He was showing me how strong he was," Homan remembers. "I knew he was telling me that he could kill me with his bare hands if he could get at me. I looked at him, and I laughed and walked on by."

On February 24 the word flashed that Gwen Burton was about to testify. The Minnesota media had promised that they would not reveal her identity when they covered the day's events; her testimony would reveal such intimate details that printing her name would only add to the burden she carried.

Slowly the tiny dark-haired woman walked toward the witness stand and placed her hand on the Bible to take the oath. She did not look at the defendant, nor did he look at her. Instead, he stared at his hands.

Glaeser led her through the questioning gently. She said she was—or had been—a second-year nursing student when the attack occurred. She had been a swimmer, a skier, and she had played touch football. "But I can't do any of those things now."

Her voice was almost too soft to be heard as she began what would be a two-hour-long ordeal. She was very nervous, and she swiveled the witness chair as she testified.

"He stopped to help me in the Sears parking lot because my car wouldn't start, and he invited me home with him to get some tools. I didn't say anything and he started looking real mean, like he was mad. I was frightened, and I went with him."

The room full of strangers listened raptly, waiting to hear every word of what was excruciatingly intimate testimony, especially for a girl who had had no sexual experience before encountering the defendant.

Resolutely Gwen Burton told of being forced to perform fellatio three times, of submitting to sexual fondling at the hands of the man who held her captive. She told of being choked and punched in the stomach.

"He told me to sit on the blanket. The last time I remember seeing him was when I turned around and I saw him walking behind the car with a hammer in his hand. . . ."

And then she testified that she could not remember anything until she woke up in the deep gully about forty feet away from where the blanket had been, and found that she was lying in a pool of blood.

"At first I was just going to lie back down and go to sleep. Then I remembered my sister had called me that morning and said she was pregnant, and I wanted to see the baby, so I decided I'd better try to get help."

Gwen described crawling for over three hours on her hands and knees, stopping to rest every two or three feet. "I just thought about getting to see my sister's baby, and finishing school."

Glaeser asked her to evaluate what her physical injuries had been, and she responded by saying that she knew the left side of her skull had been fractured and that bone fragments had been driven into her brain. Her right arm and leg were completely paralyzed for a while, she said, and that side was still weak.

"My sense of balance is returning, but when I'm tired, I have trouble speaking."

Cross-examination of an appealing victim is always dangerous territory for a defense attorney, but Douglas Thomson attempted to get Gwen Burton to say that Harvey's conversation had been rambling and disoriented, that his eyes had been transfixed and staring.

She did not remember that that had been true. "He only said once that people think he is crazy because he believes in God."

"Do *you* think Mr. Carignan is crazy?" Thomson asked bluntly.

Gwen answered clearly and firmly, "No, I don't—no."

The prosecution's objection was sustained. Clearly this called for a conclusion by the witness, who was not an expert in psychiatry. Judge Haering ordered the jury to disregard the question and answer.

And finally Gwen's ordeal was over and she was allowed to step down. She took a seat in the gallery, determined to watch the legal procedure that would, she hoped, see Harvey Carignan convicted.

Now the defense's case began. Had Prosecutor Glaeser attempted to call June Lynch, a victim in another case, as a witness in *this* case, he would have, under ordinary circumstances, been blocked by outraged cries from the defense. But this was not an ordinary defense game plan. In Friedberg's and Thomson's plan to show that Harvey Carignan was a raving, frothing paranoid-schizophrenic, June Lynch might be a plus. They gambled that she would help them show that Harvey was so bad, so evil, that he *had* to be crazy.

June told the jury that Harvey had picked up her and her friend Lisa King, on September 8 and driven them to where "his son's truck had run out of gas" near Mora, Minnesota.

"I walked with him into the woods where the truck was supposed to be, and the next thing I remember is waking up in the back of a deputy's car.

"I don't remember how many times he hit me with the hammer. The doctors told me later that it was at least seven times—maybe more."

Thomson continued to call witnesses that might be expected to appear on the other side of the case. His next witness was Minneapolis Homicide Detective Lieutenant Russel Krueger. Krueger had interrogated Harvey on September 25 after his arrest.

"Did you have a religious discussion with Harvey Carignan?" Thomson asked.

"I asked him if he believed in Jesus Christ," Krueger answered. "And if he did, why did he not have a conscience?

He said, 'Judge not, lest ye be judged.' And then he started giving me Bible verses.''

Krueger's opinion of the defendent was succinct: "I have never talked to anyone so cold, so evil as this man. He certainly is possessed by the devil, in my opinion.''

Could "possessed by the devil" be construed as legally insane? The defense apparently hoped it could.

The courtroom and the jury were going to have a chance to judge for themselves. Thomson and Friedberg called Harvey Louis Carignan to the witness stand.

He rose from his chair at the defense table and ambled to the witness chair. He wore, not a proper suit and tie as most murder defendants do, but an open-necked sport shirt over a white T-shirt, his great shoulders stretching the fabric.

Harvey Carignan was going was going to tell his own story.

15

Joseph Friedberg began the direct examination of Harvey Carignan. "Will you state your full name, please?"

Harvey answered in a polite, clear voice. His thick fingers were laced together in his lap. He might have been a humble truck driver, someone's kind neighbor testifying as a witness—instead of the defendant in a vicious rape trial.

"Harvey Louis Carignan."

"How old are you, Mr. Carignan."

"Forty-seven."

"When were you born?"

"May 18, 1927."

"Where?"

"Fargo, North Dakota."

"What is the extent of your education?"

"I have a high-school education, and I have some college."

"Where did you get the college?"

"Penitentiaries."

"Which penitentiaries?"

"Several."

"Can you name them?"

"McNeil Island, Alcatraz, Leavenworth, Walla Walla."

"Have you been sitting here and listening to the testimony?"

"Not too much."

"You understand that the defense in this case is mental illness?"

"I do."

"*Are* you crazy?"

"No."

Glaeser objected at this point, citing that this question called for a conclusion that the witness was not qualified to give.

"No one is more competent to testify to this than the defendant," Friedberg countered, and then agreed to withdraw the question.

"Do you feel you are mentally ill?"

"No."

"Then why are you permitting the defense on mental illness to be used in this courtroom?"

"Makes no difference what defense they use."

"You heard the testimony of Gwen Burton, did you not?"

"Some of it."

"Are you the man that did the things she claimed?"

"I was the man that was with her. I didn't do everything she claimed."

"Did you do some things that she didn't talk about?"

"That's hard to answer. . . . The things that happened— she said happened—did happen, but not always for the reasons she said."

"Why did you stop and pick Gwen Burton up that day?"

"God told me to."

"When?"

"When I was by her car."

"What were you doing by her car?"

"I had stopped to help her start her car."

"You heard her testify, did you not, that you claimed that you had asked God for the ability to help somebody that day. Is that true?"

"I didn't hear her testify that, but I did, yes."

"Did you hear that?"

"Yes, I did."

"Did you intend to help her?"

"Yes, when I stopped."

"Then what happened?"

"I was looking under the hood, and God told me she was a whore."

"He told you she was a *what?*"

"A whore."

"How did God tell you that?"

"Just talked to me and just told me."

"Does God talk to you frequently?"

"Yes, quite frequently."

"Any particular time or place?"

"No."

"How do you know it is God?"

"I just know it is."

"Well, all you know is it is a voice, don't you?"

"That's right."

"How do you know that?"

"I just know it is."

"Did you intend to kill her?"

"Yes."

"When did you form the intent to kill her?"

"When God told me to kill her."

"When was that?"

"Just before I killed her, or tried to kill her."

"Did anybody tell you to do all those other things?"

"Yes."

"Who told you that?"

"God told me that."

"This voice?"

Harvey was annoyed; he had tried to make it plain to this clod of a lawyer who was questioning him. *"God!"*

"Where does it come from?"

Harvey lifted his hand to point upward. "Comes from up in the air."

"Have you discussed this type of thing with people before?"

"What kind of thing?"

"Well, you have heard the testimony where somebody indicated that you had said that people thought that you might be off the track for being so religious—as you are—did you say that to Gwen Burton?"

"Yes."

"What people think you are off the track?"

"Friends—some of my relatives."

"How was your relationship with your relatives?"

"Not good."

"Do you have any friends?"

"I have acquaintances."

"I take it to mean you do—or do not—have friends?"

"All depends on what you call a friend. I don't have any close friends."

"Well, you found out now—you found out quite soon afterwards that you didn't kill her. What was your reaction to that?"

"I was sorry."

"What do you mean, you were sorry?"

"I was sorry I didn't kill her."

A slight wave of sound rippled through the courtroom, and eyes turned toward Gwen Burton, who sat listening, fascinated as one might be when caught in the gaze of a poisonous snake.

"Why?" prompted Friedberg.

"Because I was supposed to."

"Well, you saw some testimony, or I don't know if you heard it or not, but there was testimony in this courtroom that there were some scratches and cuts on her chest. Do you know how they got there?"

"I didn't put them there myself."

"Did you drag her?"

"Yes."

"Where did you drag her to?"

"I drug her from the side of the car, over to the top of the gully, and gave her a pull, and she slid down."

"And then what did you do?"

"I left."

"Did you stay there at all?"

"No, I stayed there a little bit before, but not after that."

"Did you think she was dead?"

"Yes."

"Why didn't you hit her to make sure?"

"God didn't say to mutilate her. He just said to hit her until she was dead."

Archie Sonenstahl and Duane Homan exchanged glances. They had seen this man always in full command of his senses, and they each knew what the other was thinking. Harvey was putting on one hell of an act.

"You heard a young lady—I don't know if you heard her or not—but you were in the courtroom when June Lynch testified?"

"I know her."

"Have you ever seen her before?"

"I have."

"Did you hit her with a hammer?"

"I did."

"Was there any of this degrading conduct that went on before that?"

"No."

"She testified that it seemed to be that she was walking through the woods, and she doesn't remember anything after that. Is that consistent with what you did?"

"Yes."

"How many times did you hit her?"

"Nine or ten."

"Did you believe she was dead?"

"Yes."

"There was another girl waiting in the cab [sic] at this time, wasn't there?"

"Yes."

"That was your car?"

"Yes."

"What were your plans for her?"

"I was going to kill her."

"How?"

"Same way."

"Why?"

"Because God told me to."

"Why had God wanted you to kill those ladies?"

"I don't know," Harvey replied calmly. "I never asked him."

"Did God tell you anything about these two girls as to whether or not they were whores?"

"Yes, he did."

"What did he say?"

"He just told me they were whores, and to take them somewhere and kill them."

"Now, outside of these situations where God has told you to do these things, do you talk to God about other things?"

"Lots of things. Yes."

"Has God talked back to you?"

"Yes."

"Always?"

"No—not always. Sometimes He doesn't answer."

There was a nervous giggle somewhere in the courtroom. The energy generated by the defendant's testimony was tremendous, and at the same time, the spectators had begun to feel that they had entered into another dimension, a dimension of madness.

"You have to wait for a response sometimes?" Friedberg continued.

"Sometimes He doesn't answer."

"You know why that is?"

"No."

"Have you ever *seen* God?"

"Yes."

"On how many occasions?"

"Hundreds."

"How do you know it is God?"

"I just know."

"When have you seen Him?"

"The last time?"

"Yes."

"Last night."

"When you were asleep?"

"No. Before I went to sleep."

"Were your eyes open or closed?"

"They were closed last night."

"Have you ever seen Him when your eyes were open?"

"Yes, but very seldom."

"Does He talk when you see Him?"

"Yes."

"Always?"

"He always talks at some time during the time I see Him, yes."

"Why has He chosen you to do this work?"

"I don't know. He didn't tell me."

"Have you been that good a person over your life that you should be selected for this work?"

"I don't know."

"As a matter of fact, you have been a bad person from time to time, haven't you?"

"I guess."

"You have been convicted of crimes, have you not?"

"Yes."

"Been convicted of burglary a couple of times?"

"Yes."

"Did God tell you to commit those burglaries?"

"No, He didn't."

"Why did you commit them?"

"I wanted money."

"How long ago were they?"

"Oh, one was about ten or twelve years ago, and another was about eight."

"You were also convicted of a sex crime in 1950, were you not?"

"If that's what you call it—yes."

"What happened there? Did God tell you to do that?"

"No."

"What did you do?"

Friedberg was pulling out all the stops. The question was: Would he go too far? Would the jury overlook the ploy to make Harvey look insane and focus on the crimes?

Duane Homan listened to Harvey's carefully flat tone and almost admired the way he prudently stopped short of answering more than was asked. Well, he had never claimed that Harvey was dumb or not a good actor.

Harvey continued his description of the attack twenty-six years before on Dorcas Callen, his tone and words making it all sound like a mistake anyone might have made.

"Just went over, talked to a woman. I thought I knew her, and I didn't. I talked to her a little while and we had some words about something and I grabbed her and we fell down in a hole and I helped her out and we walked back to where my three friends were, and we talked there maybe a minute or so, and pretty soon she just started running across the street.''

Good one, Harv, Homan thought. You just summed up a whole attempted rape in one sentence.

"Were you at that time in your life hearing God talk to you?'' Friedberg asked.

"Not at that time, no.''

"Had you ever seen God at that time?''

"Yes, I had before, yes.''

"How—you admit that you did these things—you don't admit that you assaulted that woman back in 1949?''

Harvey explained patiently, "Not in the sense that they said I did, no.''

"What happened to you?''

"What happened to what?''

"What happened to you because of that contact with that woman?''

"I went to jail for fifteen years.''

"What jails did you go to?''

"McNeil Island, and from there I went to Alcatraz.''

"All right. And you deny that you assaulted that woman in 1949?''

"Yeah. I deny that I assaulted her in the sense that they said I did, yes.''

"Did you assault her in any sense?''

"Well, I shouldn't have pushed her. No, I shouldn't have, so I did.''

Friedberg suddenly switched gears, backing off from the Alaska incident. "Can you describe what God looks like?''

"Yes and no.''

"Go ahead and try.''

"Well, He stands up and He talks and holds His hands out like this . . .'' Harvey stood up and demonstrated God's stance to the jury and the courtroom. "And He has got a hood on and you can't see His face, and His feet have kind of like slippers with thongs on them, and they go around the top of His feet and up His legs.''

"You are telling this jury, and everybody here, that God tells you to kill?"

"That's right."

"Suppose I tell you that God doesn't tell people to kill?"

"I'd tell you that you are lying."

"Why?"

"Because He told *me* to."

"Harvey, if you were to die, do you believe you would go to Heaven?"

"I know I would go to Heaven."

"How do you know?"

"I just know I would. According to the Bible, I would go to Heaven, that's all."

"Do you read the Bible?"

"All the time."

"In addition to God telling you to do these things, does the Bible tell you that you are right?"

"Yes."

"Could you give me an example of how?"

"Well, I could probably give you several. The one that comes to mind is in Colossians."

"What does it say?"

"To mortify, rid yourself of these people."

"Does it say *which* people?"

"Yes."

"Which people?"

"Whores and harlots, and people of the like."

"Do you believe that there are a lot of these people around?"

"Yes, I believe so."

"Can you tell by looking at them?"

"No."

"When you do these things, is there any change? Do you become strong or not?"

"What do you mean—strong?"

"Are you a strong person?"

"Yes, I am very strong."

"Does it ever cross your mind that you are wrong?"

Harvey appeared bemused. "*Wrong* to do these things?"

"Yes."

"No—that's not wrong."

"Do you know what a devil spirit is?"

"I have heard of them."

"Do you believe they exist?"

"I believe the devil exists."

"What is a devil spirit?"

"I don't know. It's just something I have heard of since I have been locked up."

"Has somebody told you or have you considered the fact that this isn't God you are talking to—that it's the devil spirit?"

"I have had a lot of people tell me it was the devil spirit."

"Why don't you believe them?"

"Because it didn't look like the devil. He looked like God."

"Did you ever know what God looked like before you saw this?"

"Yes."

"How?"

"He has always looked the same ever since I have been a little kid."

"How old were you when you first saw Him?"

"I was less than four."

"Do you remember the circumstances?"

"Yes. I would . . . didn't say my prayers. He was watching me, and I got out of bed and said them, and He left."

"All right. Have you been saved?"

"Yes."

"When?"

"About the middle of July—last year."

"How did that happen?"

"I was going to a Bible school and I was at home getting ready to go, and I was reading from the Gospel of John, and Jesus was telling His disciples how to be saved, and I sat down and I believed real hard and I was saved."

"Have you spoken in tongues?"

"Yes."

"What does that mean to you?"

"It means I am talking with God."

"You understand what you are saying?"

"No I don't."

"Does God understand?"

"Yes."

"How do you know?"

"Because He answers."

"Harvey—Mr. Carignan—are you at all sorry that you have done this?"

Harvey looked incredulous. "No."

"You understand that you are in a courtroom and that you are being tried for doing it, right?"

"Yes, I understand that."

"You know it is against the law of the State of Minnesota, do you not?"

"Yeah."

"Then why isn't it wrong?"

"Because God's law becomes above man's law. If you have to break man's law to give God's law, you have to do it."

Whether Harvey was out-and-out crazy was questionable, Homan realized. But he was certainly faultless on the stand. Attorneys always rehearse their witnesses, throwing questions at them before trial that may or may not be asked when they reach the witness stand, trying to break them out of sight of the jury. And then they can pick up the pieces, reminding their witnesses that they must be prepared for the worst. The most important advice is always, "Never answer more than is asked; never volunteer."

Harvey was sticking to his yeses and nos and keeping his responses to simple sentences. Homan knew this must be difficult for Harvey, who had always shown that he had definite opinions. And he figured Harvey had to be scared; otherwise, his ego would never have permitted an insanity defense.

It looked as if Harvey preferred being thought loony as a jaybird to being sent back inside the walls. Well, he'd said he was never going back.

Friedberg was now leading Harvey through the story of his life. The questioning went smoothly until the attorney asked

Harvey to verify that his mother had sexually abused him when he was just a child.

"Did your mother do the things you heard about?"

"I don't want to talk about it."

"You understand that we have got to tell this jury your entire background?"

"Yeah."

"Will you talk about it?"

"When I told you that stuff, I told you that in confidence."

"All right. You heard about an incident with a baby-sitter?"

"Yes."

"What happened?"

"She used to take me and she would rub herself all over me."

"Did that bother you?"

"Yeah."

"Why?"

"I don't know. I just felt it wasn't right."

Friedberg continued to paint the picture of the abused and abandoned child, working tediously through Harvey's many changes of residences as a child, on through his years at Mandan and his years in the Army. The prison years were skipped over as lightly as if they were only incidental, rather than the major portion of the defendant's life.

Harvey's voice faltered and blurred as he recalled his first marriage, and his disappointment in Sheila. He related his scarlet, blind rage when Sheila had failed to help him in his carpentry project, and the long night's wait while he clutched the hammer, waiting to kill her. This was good stuff; this would help to solidify the insanity plea, show that Harvey had been obsessed with vengeance via hammer for many years.

Friedberg asked about the second marriage, Harvey's marriage to Alice.

"What happened then?"

"I had a business then. I had a service station and a garage, and I had some problems come up, and my wife went over to her mother's house, and she never came back, and I thought that she had left me, and I found out later that they had held her there for three days and wouldn't let her go, so I just took off.''

Harvey was not asked what his "problems" were in Seattle, and he certainly did not mention the investigation into Kathy Miller's disappearance and murder. Instead, he sounded sincere as he lied and claimed that Alice's family had kept her from him, although he surely knew that Alice had hidden from him in terror.

"Where did you come to, Minnesota?"

"I came to Minnesota, and went back to Washington in about a week, and we could not agree on anything, and I came back here.''

"Did you ever get told to kill *her*?" (Alice Carignan.)

"No—but told to hit her.''

"Did you?"

"Yes."

"How hard?"

"Pretty hard.''

"With what?"

"My fists.''

"Was that when you got back together with her?"

"No, once it was before then, and I hit her, and cut her lip here . . . [he raised one hand to indicate where he had injured Alice] and the other time was when I went back, we were talking about it. I had been driving my pickup and she had my Toronado, and I wanted her to use that around town, and she said yes, and so I was going out to the car with her, and she bent over to get into the car, and I just hit her.''

So much for Heloise and Abelard, Romeo and Juliet . . . Harvey's second marriage now sounded more like "The Bickersons.''

Friedberg sensed that this last information had not set well with the jury, and he once again changed the thrust of his questioning.

"Harvey, when did you find out about The Way Ministry International?"

"About April last year.''

"What did you do in relation to that?"

"I started going to what they call Twig Meetings.''

"What is a Twig Meeting?"

"A meeting where people get together and talk about the Word, and somebody teaches you from the Bible."

"Did you get what you wanted out of these meetings?"

"Oh yes."

"How did you come to feel about The Way Ministry?"

"I really liked it. I felt that the people in there were the only people in my life that I had ever met who really believed, and, you know, really lived according to the Word, and really tried to walk the way Jesus Christ walked the earth."

"Do you believe you live the way Jesus Christ did?"

"Yes."

"He didn't hit any women, did he?"

"I don't know."

"When you were talking to Lieutenant Krueger, did you try to save him?"

"Yes."

"Why?"

"I thought he needed saving."

"What made you think that?"

Harvey's answer brought guffaws to the tense courtroom. "I think all policemen need saving."

"Lieutenant Krueger treated you badly?"

"No."

"How about any of the other policemen? Did you try to save them?

"Yes . . . they wouldn't listen."

There was a short court recess, and Homan and Sonenstahl discussed whether Harvey's "crazy" act was working. The gallery seemed to be buying it, and Glaeser appeared dumbfounded that the defense would attempt such a dramatic bid for innocent by reason of insanity.

"I know Harv," Homan told Sonenstahl. "He may look crazy up there, and he may sound crazy, but he knows what he's doing."

Sonenstahl nodded. "We've got the papers he wrote in prison on paranoia and the sexual criminal. He got A's. He researched the symptoms carefully. He might as well have written his own script for this."

"Harvey will get up there and froth at the mouth and dance like a monkey if that's what it takes," Homan said bitterly. "I'm curious to see the next act. But, Archie . . . I am disappointed about one thing."

"What's that?"

"That you wouldn't listen when Harv was trying to save you; it's the least you could have done."

Sonenstahl laughed shortly and they walked back into the courtroom.

16

When court resumed, Joseph Friedberg returned to his precise questioning of Harvey.

"Can you explain to me why, if God told you to kill Gwen Burton, you committed all these sexual acts upon her first?"

"He told me to humiliate her first."

"Did He tell you—He told you to humiliate her—did He also tell you you were going to have to kill her?"

"No."

"Prior to hitting her with that hammer, did you do something?"

"You mean just before?"

"Yes."

"Yes, she was laying on a blanket, and I was sitting beside her, and I fixed her hair."

"Why did you fix her hair?"

"I just wanted her to look nice."

"For what?"

"When she went before God for judgment."

"I thought you said she was a whore."

"I did."

"You still wanted her to look nice?"

"Yes."

"Why?"

"I don't know."

"Harvey, what part of the Bible is it that talks about this mortification and humiliation?"

"It is in several places. I was thinking of the Colossians."

"Do you have a Bible with you?"

"Always." Harvey reached into the pocket of his sports shirt and produced a small Bible.

"Could you find it?"

"I think so, if I can read it." He frowned, as if trying to decipher the small print. "I can't read it."

"You say third chapter of Colossians?"

"Colossians Three."

"I will read it to you and you tell me if that's what you referred to. 'Mortify therefore your members which are upon the earth: fornication, uncleanliness, inordinate affection, evil concupiscence, and covetousness, which is idolatry.' Is that what you are referring to?"

"That's what I am referring to."

"That justifies God's order to you in relation to Gwen?"

"It does according to the Bible. I would listen to God even if I hadn't read any of this."

Friedberg ended his direct examination.

Now it was Prosecutor William Glaeser's turn to cross-examine this man who stolidly claimed that God was responsible for all his crimes against women. Carignan maintained his humble, righteous demeanor, but Homan, watching, caught a glint of wariness in the defendant's eyes as Glaeser moved to a position in front of the witness stand.

There was only the faintest trace of sarcasm in Glaeser's voice as he began his questioning.

"You say, Mr. Carignan, that you saw God for the first time when you were less than four years old. Is that correct?"

"That's right."

"You didn't see Him again until you were married and living out in Seattle, Washington, with your first wife?"

"No, that's not what I said. I said I saw Him the first time when I was about less than four years old, and I saw Him many, many times about that time, and then I didn't see Him again until—"

"Many times when you were approximately four years old?"

"Four or five . . . six."

"Then during this period of time that you were in reform

school, and in and out of prison and in the service, you didn't see him at all?''

"No, I didn't.''

"And you didn't see Him again until you were so mad at your wife that you saw red and you looked up and at that time was when God told you to kill her?''

"A little bit after that, yes.''

"The next [time] after this early appearance—during the appearance of God to you early in your life—the next time you saw Him was with instructions to kill someone?''

"Right.''

"To kill someone that you were, in your own words, so mad at that you had this tremendous pain in your head, and you saw red?''

"Right.''

"The next time you saw God was when He told you to hit your wife, your second wife—is that correct?''

"That's right.''

"So that started—what year was that, by the way?''

"Seventy—seventy-one, somewhere in there.''

"Back starting then in 1970 or '71, I take it that your primary visitations from God were when He gave you instructions to kill or humiliate some women?''

"That's right.''

"How *many* women has He given you instructions to kill and humiliate since that time?''

"To kill *and* humiliate?''

"To kill and humiliate.''

"Four.''

"These instances, you—strike that . . . How many did He give you instructions to kill?''

"I think the answer should have been five . . . four instances . . . three.''

Harvey looked discomfited; he was trying to compute in his head how many victims he should be mentioning.

"Three? To kill three?'' Glaeser prompted.

"Yes.''

"Including Gwen Burton?''

"Including Gwen Burton.''

"How many times just to humiliate women?"

"Just once."

"Mr. Carignan, who witnessed you into The Way?"

"A girl by the name of Eileen Hunley."

Joseph Friedberg started to rise to his feet; the turf was becoming treacherous.

"When did you meet Eileen Hunley?" Glaeser continued, expecting that the ax was about to fall from the defense table.

"About January of last year."

"What kind of a relationship did you have with Eileen Hunley?"

"Your Honor!" Friedberg shouted. "Objection. It is our intent to claim the Fifth Amendment for Mr. Carignan. He stands on that right."

Judge Haering summoned the attorneys to his bench for a conversation out of the hearing of the jury.

Friedberg argued under his breath. "He is talking about a case that there is some probable cause for murder in the first degree. He has a right not to answer. It is a separate case. We didn't go into that instance, and he is not going to incriminate himself."

Glaeser argued that this area had, indeed, been opened up in direct examination. "I intend to establish that Eileen Hunley became not only a good friend, but that she was considered his girlfriend, and I would then ask him when was the last time he saw her, what she was doing. . . ."

Friedberg asked for a mistrial, as Carignan had not yet been charged with murder in the death of Eileen Hunley, and because he had had to claim immunity from answering by invoking the Fifth Amendment in front of the jury.

Judge Haering denied the motion for a mistrial, but he would not allow Glaeser to continue his line of questioning about Eileen Hunley either.

Glaeser turned back to Harvey, who sat waiting patiently on the witness stand, his hand rising to touch the Bible in his pocket from time to time.

"Referring specifically to the Gwen Burton case, you have indicated that you did, as she alleged, meet her in the parking lot of Sears on Lake Street?"

"That's right."

"And apparently you had admitted that various sexual activities that she has testified to were in fact committed by you?"

"That's right."

"And apparently it is also your admission in court that when you struck her on the head with the hammer, you intended to cause her death?"

"Right."

"That was a premeditated act, determined by you prior to the actual striking, executed with the intent of causing death?"

"God told me to do it, yes."

"You *intended* to cause her death?"

"Right."

"How many times have you failed to carry out God's command to cause death?"

"Three times."

"You have failed to carry it out three times?"

"Right. Three people—two occasions."

"Three people on two separate occasions, is that correct?"

"That's right."

"Whenever you received the command in other instances, you carried it out?"

"That's right."

"Mr. Carignan, do you know what the law of the State of Minnesota was with regard to sexually attacking a nonconsenting female at the time you carried on this assault?"

Friedberg tensed but said nothing.

"Did I know what the law was?" Harvey asked.

"Yes."

"I knew there was a law against it."

"You knew there was a law against the sexual attack on this girl that you did?"

"Right."

"Did you know that there was a law against killing her?"

"Yes."

"So that at the time that you committed the crime, you intentionally and knowingly sexually assaulted her and attempted to cause her death?"

"I never gave the law any thought."

Homan glanced at the jury, trying for the hundredth, thousandth time in his long career as a law officer to gauge their feelings from their faces. It was an impossible task; their eyes were turned toward Harvey, and they were listening avidly. The man had just admitted sodomy and attempted murder, and admitted it even as he said he had not given the law a thought. In a juror's mind, did this make him insane or a monster without conscience?

"You have also indicated—or your counsel indicated—that you felt so badly about failing in that command to kill Gwen Burton that even today if you were in a position to do so, you would carry it out and finish the job that you started on September 14. Is that correct?"

"Yes . . . I think I would have to."

Gwen Burton, sitting in the courtroom, listened as Carignan said he would still kill her—if only he had the chance.

". . . In other words, this command isn't something that you received from God in some sort of vision or something, and then it leaves you, but something that stays with you?"

"It has been renewed."

"So your command to kill Gwen Burton has been renewed by God, is that it?"

"That's right."

"When was it last renewed?"

"Last night."

"You were pretty angry with her for not dying. Is that right?"

"That's right."

"You were pretty angry for her not dying, because it was her testimony and her information to the police that led to your arrest?"

"No."

"That makes no difference to you?" Glaeser let disbelief slide into his tone.

"It makes none."

"God, in fact, is becoming an easy out for you on every instance that you have violated the law, hasn't He?"

Harvey's voice became, if anything, more pious and more

humble. "I think I know what you are saying, and I think the answer is no—if I understand you."

"You have just indicated that you are satisfied that you are going to go to heaven regardless of how many criminal acts you may have committed during your life?"

"No, not how many adult—you confuse me—talking about criminal acts and other things that we were talking about. I would just like to be sure I know what you are talking about."

"Do you believe in the Bible?"

Harvey smiled. This was his area. "Right."

"And is it not true that the word of God teaches that you are to obey civil law as well as the word of God?"

"I think it says something about rendering those things unto Caesar that is Caesar's and those things unto God that are God's."

"In other words, you are to render the due respect to the civil law as required by the civil law. Isn't that true?"

"Well, yes, but in that respect it also says that the Word and everything in it belongs to the Lord."

"But you acknowledge that there is a civil law and that the Bible that you read so frequently instructs you to obey that civil law and pay attention to it?"

"Yes."

"All right. Do you agree with me then also that a violation of that civil law, in disregard of that law, constitutes the commission of a crime under the law?"

Now Harvey had the picture, and he responded with the same litany. "Not if God's law comes first. God's law always comes first."

"Is *that* what you think the Bible says?"

"That is what I *know* it says."

"Okay. All right. So regardless of what the Bible says, under civil law a violation of that law is made a crime, is it not?"

"You made a charge and I pleaded guilty to it. I have admitted doing the charge."

"And it's your opinion that you are not mentally ill?"

"No, I'm not mentally ill."

"You are in full control of your faculties and always have been?"

"I think so, yes."

It was such a clever convoluted defense, and Harvey was giving an Oscar-winning performance. Blame it all on God, admit to everything, and then insist that you are sane—and the jury will think you are a shoo-in for the Home for the Bewildered.

Glaeser tapped a file of papers on his table.

"During the period that you were incarcerated, did you take some sociology courses?"

"Yes, I did."

"Where was that?"

"Walla Walla, Washington."

Harvey admitted that he had taken several college-level courses in the Washington State Penitentiary.

"And as part of that course, were you required to write papers on various subjects?"

"Yes."

"Did you, in fact, receive quite excellent grades in that sociology course?"

"I did."

"And were some of the papers that you wrote there on topics such as the well-adjusted man?"

Harvey tensed a little and then said, "I don't remember, but it's possible, yes."

"How about a paper on the sexual psychopath?"

"It's possible."

"And the paranoid?"

"It's possible."

The prosecutor let the subject of Carignan's expertise in the symptoms and manifestations of mental illness sink into the jury's minds and then moved on to discuss the defendant's criminal record in detail. It was interesting that Harvey, the alleged paranoid schizophrenic, had perfect recall of dates, times, and places in his life from the age of four to the present.

And then, for the first time in his hours on the stand, he showed emotion—when he discussed the failure of his marriage to Alice. All of his letters, calls, and trips back to Seattle had ended in her ultimate rejection of him. Only then were his words choked. He had told Alice of his passion for certainty, his obsession to know that she did, indeed, still love him. All in vain.

Now Glaeser smoothly brought up the subject of Harvey's education again.

"You indicated that you did obtain a high-school diploma during the period of time that you were in prison. Is that correct?

"That's right."

"How many credits of college work did you take altogether?"

"I don't have any idea."

"How many courses did you take?"

"I think that I only took one or two accredited courses. The rest I just took like in a classroom or just reading."

"And in the courses that you actually took as accredited courses, were you graded on the work that you did during that period of time?"

"Yes."

"What kind of grades did you achieve in the accredited courses?"

"I think in sociology . . . I think I got a straight A."

"What other accredited courses did you take?"

"I don't remember right now. I think it was—I don't know what it was called—something to do with newspaper work."

"It was an accredited college-level course?"

"Yes, but I don't know if I ever got the credit."

"How was your grade in that course?"

"About a C, I think."

The next question was spat into the air with the force of a hand slapping down on the bar. "What position was Gwen Burton in when you struck her with the hammer?"

Harvey answered in a tone as calm as he had used when he explained he had gotten a C in journalism. "She was laying flat on her stomach, with her arms out in front of her with the left side of her face out like this." He demonstrated to the jury.

"Had you instructed her to lie that way?"

"Yes."

"Was she fully clothed at that time?"

"Yes she was."

"Did you hear her testimony this morning that when she came to, her sweater was lying alongside of her?"

"I did."

"How did that occur?"

"When she was sliding down this embankment into the ditch, or whatever, her things just rolled up and came off."

"Why did you drag her from the location where you struck her with the hammer to the point in the ditch where she came to?"

"I wanted to hide her."

"You wanted to hide her, you didn't want people to find her?"

"Probably, yes."

"You didn't want people to find her because that might lead to you?"

"That's possibly right, yes."

"And you didn't want this to lead to you because when you hit her on the head with that hammer, you knew it was wrong?"

"When I hit her on the head with the hammer, I never thought about it. I thought about it afterwards that it was illegal, not wrong."

Harvey Carignan's understanding of the law was most precise. He obviously knew about the M'Naughton Rule—that the perpetrator of a crime cannot be excused because of mental illness unless he did not perceive that his crime was wrong at the moment it took place.

"It was illegal. You thought about it?"

"Afterwards."

"And you recognized that, and for that purpose you attempted to hide the body?"

"That's right."

"I have no other questions."

Defense Attorney Friedberg stood up for redirect examination, ready to attempt to mitigate the impression left after

Harvey had coldly described how he threw away the body—
what he thought was the corpse—of Gwen Burton.

"Mr. Carignan, is God with you?"

"Yes, He is."

"How do you know?"

"Because I received the Holy Spirit."

"Can you feel Him with you?"

"Do you mean like something moving, or something like
that?"

"How do you know He is with you?"

"Just feel him, he feels good."

"You feel good?"

"Yes."

"Ever had any doubt in your mind that He is with you?"

"No."

"I have no questions."

Friedberg sat down. If Harvey had succeeded in convincing
the jury that he was a religious nut, pushed over the edge of
the far side of sanity, he would have carried off the greatest
scam since Sinclair Lewis' Elmer Gantry had roved the Midwest seducing maidens and gathering a fortune in the name of
God.

Prosecutor Glaeser's sarcasm was pungent and heavy as he
rose again to question Harvey on recross. Harvey regarded
him quietly, his lined face still.

"Mr. Carignan, has God ever given you an order to do a
legal act?"

"Talked to me to do things?"

"You have testified that he had ordered you to do these
things that you have testified to here in court. God—"

"Objection!" Friedberg cried. "It is beyond the scope of
redirect!"

"I don't mind answering," Harvey said softly.

"I will permit him to answer this question," Judge Haering
ruled.

"He has directed me at certain times to read out of the
Bible to testify to people, and that sort of thing."

"You have indicated also that you don't like prison?"

"I really didn't indicate I don't like it; it is immaterial."

"Counsel just asked you whether your being in prison bothered you—didn't you say just now that you don't like it?"

"I meant in the sense that I don't like it any more than I like anything."

"You would rather not go back?"

"It doesn't make any difference. Whatever God wants, that's what I will do."

"You feel that because you have received God, or received the Lord as you indicated, that you therefore have forgiveness for any acts that you committed?"

"Come again?"

Glaeser repeated his question, slowly.

"Absolutely." Harvey nodded.

"And that's why in spite of recognizing that you have done these things to this girl, you can sit there and say that you feel good just because you know, or feel in your mind that you are forgiven?"

"You talk like the devil himself," Harvey responded scathingly.

"Is that what you believe?"

"Do I believe that you are the devil? I believe that you work for him."

"Do you believe that you have forgiveness?"

"Yes!"

"That regardless of what you have done to this girl, you have been forgiven?"

Harvey looked puzzled. "Forgiven for *what*?"

"For what you did to her."

"*There is nothing to be forgiven for.*"

Harvey Carignan's remarkable testimony was over. Gwen Burton shivered. The man who had beaten her with a hammer until she thought she was dying had just said there was nothing for him to regret or repent, that he would happily finish the job if he could get at her.

She did a little praying of her own—that the jury would not believe his insanity act. And then she ran from the courtroom.

Duane Homan and Archie Sonenstahl shrugged into their coats and walked from the old courthouse in Chaska into the bitter-cold air of a Minnesota February. Each man was shaking his head unconsciously.

"Did he pull it off?" Sonenstahl asked his compatriot from Seattle.

"He sounded crazy as a bedbug, didn't he?"

"The hell with it. Let's go have a drink."

Back in his cell, Harvey Carignan ate his dinner, and then he began to work out, pulling himself up again and again to chin on the bars that comprised his inner cage. His muscles bulged as he did two dozen chin-ups.

And then he sat on the edge of his bunk to read his Bible.

17

Harvey Carignan's trial would now become a war between psychiatrists. Was he crazy? Or was he only devilishly clever?

Dr. Hector Zeller, former medical director of the Hastings State Hospital, took the stand on February 26; he would speak for the defense. He attempted to explain to the confused jury how a man could be so clever in abducting young women, and so cruel when he had them alone—and still be innocent of his crimes against them because he was psychotic.

In response to the defense attorney's prompting, Dr. Zeller set out to give the jury a crash course in insanity as it applies to murder. He recounted his impression of Harvey Carignan.

"He did not know that it was wrong. He was suffering from a defect of reason. I do feel that Mr. Carignan is mentally ill. He believes that he is an ambassador of God and his mission was to kill certain young women.

"He loved his mother," Zeller told the jury, "but he also hated her because she rejected him, punished him. He did not want to kill his mother because God would not approve. So he transferred the hate to other women. To complete the triangle, he had to develop a way not to blame himself for his acts, and the way he chose to do this was to have God order him to do these things. He has it made, because God has assured him he's going to heaven."

The explanation was a classic Freudian scenario. Was the huge man who had confessed to murderous violence really only the extension of the small boy who had tried vainly to win his mother's love, and who had lost her to a stepfather and to half-brothers who were allowed to remain at home with her—while he was sent away to reform school?

Zeller, who said he had interviewed Harvey for two and a half hours in his cell in the Carver County Jail, testified that he had had sufficient information to form his diagnosis. He said he had found a flatness in emotion in his subject, but that this deadness had fallen away when two topics were introduced: Harvey's mother and Laura Showalter's murder. Actually, it hadn't been Laura Showalter's death almost three decades before that upset Harvey—but the fact that he had been sentenced to hang in the aftermath.

"Only when he talked about rejection would emotion come, tears would show," Dr. Zeller commented. "When he talked about his mother, the tears came."

Dr. Zeller testified too that there was a history of mental illness in Harvey's family.

Somewhere, probably early in Harvey's life, he had learned to hate women and to react violently to sexual stimulation.

"As long as he is not with women, sexually stimulated, then he's going to be all right. Put him in a prison with men, and he's okay. You put him with a woman, get him sexually excited, and he's gone."

Dr. Zeller prophesied that Harvey would get worse as he aged. "He will deteriorate further; we will see more bizarre behavior."

It was an argument that the prosecution could hardly argue with.

Nor could they really dispute that Harvey practiced rituals in his attacks. The way he picked women up, the abduction out into deserted and lonely areas, and the final smashing again and again with a hammer were all part of the ritual for the destruction of women. Dr. Zeller confirmed that it was all part of a carefully compartmentalized plan, that all the elements had to be present to feed Harvey's particular psychotic aberration.

When William Glaeser stood to cross-examine Dr. Zeller, he asked why, if the psychiatrist felt that Harvey was speaking what he believed to be the truth when he said he was only doing God's work, he had tried to hide the body of the student nurse.

"I would say that it was part of the ritual," Zeller replied.

Glaeser asked how such a mentally ill person could act with apparent rationality at periods during the commission of a crime. And again, the answer was that it was part of the ritual.

Dr. Zeller insisted that he was convinced that Harvey was suffering from acute mental illness and that his emotions were not under his own control.

"So you don't think there's a possibility that he lied during the psychiatric examination?" Glaeser asked.

"No. Sometimes he can be relatively normal—but not when he's stimulated by a woman."

"Why would a mentally ill person first offer his victim money for sexual favors—and resort to force only after he was refused?"

The response was the same. When one is dealing with madness, there are no rules.

Dr. Zeller was a highly trained psychiatrist, a doctor who had treated hundreds of psychotics in his career. It would have taken a very clever liar to fool him.

Prosecutor Glaeser recalled Gwen Burton to the witness stand as the defense concluded its case, and questioned her as a rebuttal witness.

"Miss Burton—Gwen—you've heard Mr. Carignan testify that he fixed your hair before he hit you—so that you would be presentable when you met your Maker. Did he do that?"

"No, sir."

"He *didn't* fix your hair?"

"No. He only hit me with the hammer."

"He didn't pray with you, or testify before you—before he . . . sent you to meet God?"

"No, sir."

Harvey did not glance at the witness. Instead, he stared fixedly at the floor.

On Friday, Prosecutor Glaeser called a prosecution psychiatrist, Dr. Dennis Philander. While Philander agreed with Dr. Zeller that Harvey Carignan could be diagnosed as a

paranoid schizophrenic, he did not agree that the defendant
had lacked control over his own actions. That is, he did not
agree that Harvey was psychotic under legal definition. He
quoted statements made by the defendant that indicated that
Harvey had made an informed and conscious choice of action.

". . . his statements—'If you have to break man's law to
live by God's law, you have to do it, that's all . . .' and,
again, 'I thought it was illegal, not wrong'—indicate that he
was in control of himself," Philander explained.

Philander pointed out that Harvey had testified that God
had told him at nine-thirty A.M. that he should humiliate and
kill Gwen Burton. "That hallucination would have had impact on him for only a relatively short time. And yet he had
carried on rational conversation with his victim during the
three hours he had her captive. Sometime during that period,
the hallucination would have fallen away."

It had been one in the afternoon when Harvey lifted the
hammer to crush Gwen's skull. "He knew and was in command of his behavior and conduct. He tried to conceal the
crime. The victim asked him several times to take her home,
and he responded that it was too light outside and people
would see them, or that she would report him. At one point
he told her to stop crying because he was afraid people would
hear her. He appreciated the wrongfulness of the acts he
engaged in."

In the end, of course, it would be the lay jury who would
decide if Harvey was crazy or not. And they would have to
make this judgment without hearing anything of the murders
of Kathy Shultz or Eileen Hunley. They were not told of the
investigations into the murders of Kathy Miller and Laura
Leslie Brock far away in Washington. They had heard nothing of the maps with the cryptic red circles. Each case must
be decided upon its own merits.

They *had* heard of Harvey's years in prison. That had been
a calculated risk on the part of the defense team. The defense
had chosen to present Harvey in all his divine madness on the
witness stand. Murder defendants rarely testify in their own
behalf, because it opens them up to cross-examination by the
prosecution. But if Friedberg and Thomson had not asked

Harvey first about his former convictions, Glaeser would have done it—so that part of his past had had to be sacrificed. The defense hoped that it had made him seem a lifelong psychotic; the prosecution wagered that it had served only to portray him as a habitual criminal.

All the game plans had been played out by Monday morning, March 3, 1975. All that remained were final arguments and instructions by Judge Haering before the jury retired to debate.

There were four possible verdicts: guilty, not guilty, not guilty by reason of insanity, and not guilty by reason of insanity with homicidal tendencies. A simple "not guilty" was extremely unlikely, as Harvey had admitted the crimes. More than that, he had said he would kill Gwen Burton if he could get his hands on her again.

Either of the insanity verdicts would demand that procedures be put in motion for committing him to a mental institution. A straight guilty verdict would mean a thirty-year sentence in Stillwater Prison. However, as in every other state, thirty years would not mean thirty years in fact; technically, in Minnesota, Harvey would immediately become eligible for parole.

The final arguments, on both sides, were not geared to pleasing the defendant. He seemed not to hear; Harvey only stared blankly into space as his fate was being decided.

Prosecutor Glaeser stressed Harvey's ability to slip in and out of "psychosis," hitting hard at the fact that Harvey could maintain perfectly rational conversation up to the point of the murderous attack, and that he had taken carefully thought-out precautions to avoid discovery. He had not left the "body" out in the open, but had tossed it away in a deep gully. Had the "body" not revived and crawled for hours to get help, it would not have been discovered until it was only decayed flesh and bones.

Defense Attorney Douglas Thomson countered with the argument that Glaeser was "trying to explain a madman's actions" through logic.

"It doesn't work that way. Either you're off the track or you're not."

Thomson, at times sounding more like the prosecution than

the defense, called his client a "madman" several times during his closing arguments. At one dramatic moment he pointed at Harvey and pronounced him "that form—just a shell of a human being . . . a homicidal maniac . . . a stainless-steel schizophrenic."

Hardly the stuff that endears an attorney to his client.

But Thomson was attempting to keep Harvey out of Stillwater, outside the prison walls which he had come to hate passionately.

Thomson concluded with strong words: "Ladies and gentlemen. Harvey Carignan is a homicidal maniac and we are asking you so to find, for the protection of society and to make sure that what you have heard happened will never happen again."

Judge Haering instructed the jury that in order to find the defendant not guilty by reason of insanity, they must be convinced that he was more insane than he was sane.

A most difficult charge. Two psychiatrists with years of training and experience had not been able to agree on the degree of Harvey's psychosis. What would a jury do with that puzzle?

The jury retired at five P.M. on March 3. Shortly before ten that evening, they signaled that they had reached a verdict.

And the verdict was guilty.

Guilty of aggravated sodomy.

Guilty of attempted murder.

Harvey stared into space and betrayed no emotion at all as the verdict was read.

Gwen Burton, who had sat through every minute of testimony, breathed a sigh of relief. "I'm happy right where he is," she told the press. "I'm pleased with the outcome."

Joseph Friedberg said he was not surprised. "You could almost see it in their faces during closing arguments," he said of the jurors. "There was a pall of conviction."

Asked if the defense would continue their insanity defense in the trials yet to come, Friedberg said he thought not. "I don't think we'll try it again, because it didn't work here."

Nor would there be an appeal.

Harvey was ordered on March 7 to St. Peter State Hospital

for a presentence psychiatric examination. Physicians there subsequently diagnosed Harvey as having a "severe anti-social personality." In lay terms, this meant they had found him to be devoid of conscience or empathy for the needs of other human beings, *but not psychotic*.

Clinically, the antisocial personality suffers from a personality disorder which makes him terribly dangerous to those around him, but fully capable of making rational decisions. A deadly combination of attributes.

A St. Peter psychiatrist recommended imprisonment rather than mental treatment. There is, today, no known treatment that is effective in changing the structure of the antisocial personality. The defect is believed to originate in early childhood, usually before the age of five, and once the child is so damaged, his complete lack of compassion for others only becomes more solidly entrenched as he grows to adulthood.

Harvey Carignan fit so perfectly into the parameters of the diagnosis of antisocial personality that it might have been designed just for him. From the moment of conception, Harvey was a problem. The mores of the twenties dictated that illegitimacy was in and of itself a crime. Birth certificates were clearly stamped "Illegitimate," and Harvey bore that stigma early on.

He recalls sexual abuse. It is probable that he *was* the victim of molestation by one or more women during the first five years of his life. Beyond the alleged incidents of sexual trauma, the child Harvey was continally rejected by the one woman who should have accepted him: his own mother. He was sent to live with a series of relatives and quickly rejected by each new home he was sent to. It seemed clear to him that his mother did not want him, his aunts and uncles did not want him, and his grandmother did not want him. With each new abandonment, Harvey acted out his rage in socially unacceptable ways. He twitched, and he wet the bed, and then he stole. He has said himself that he "would be noticed." If he could not make people like him, he would be noticed because he was so *unlikable*. For Harvey, for any child, the most devastating reaction of all from other humans is complete uninterest. He *had* to be more than a cipher; he could not allow himself to become someone so unimportant that he was invisible. Harvey's family made every effort to shut him away from them. In essence, they had rendered him invisible. And that was a kind of death, the death of the self who could care for others.

Harvey began his life with no power at all. Women used him, humiliated him, and then sent him away. He turned his life inward, learning to hate instead of love. Learning fear instead of trust. Some vital part of human emotional mechanism was blunted and crushed before it could develop. Although he would eventually grow tall and strong, he would never develop compassion or empathy for another human being in any real sense. He would always be an emotional robot who was constitutionally unable to care about the needs of anyone else. He developed instead the facade of the clever, cocky loner, delighting in hurting other people with both sarcastic words and physical violence.

For the major portion of his life, Harvey Carignan was "warehoused," sent away where no one would have to deal with him. The spindly eleven-year-old was bullied and beaten by older boys in the training school, and, quite probably, subjected to more sexual abuse. He had no real childhood, he had no normal adolescence, and his adult life was spent behind prison walls. The man who finally emerged was a monster, but a monster whose facade was highly developed and refined. He was smart, and he could manipulate other people, even though he perceived other humans as if there was a solid glass wall between himself and them. He would have what he wanted, and the devil take those who didn't want him.

It is not surprising that women became his quarry; women had caused him pain, and he would cause them pain if they should be so bold as to reject him. His hatred and distrust of the baby-sitter, his mother, and the matrons at the training school expanded during the long years in prison until it included all women. Women were his enemies. Still, he was possessed of tremendous sexual drives, and he *needed* women to slake the raging fires within. He wanted young women, because he had never had young women. He married Sheila and Alice because he was still looking for a maternal figure, a mother who would cater to his every wish and accede to his demands docilely. It is significant that each of his wives had teenage daughters; each marriage promised him a mother figure as well as the opportunity to approach his nubile stepdaughters. It could not work, not in a million years. No woman could fill up the void in Harvey Carignan, and no teenager would accept the advances of a man so coarse, so crude, so frightening. There wasn't a female on earth who could accept him so totally that it would negate the rejections and humiliations suffered four decades earlier.

Each time a woman rejected or disappointed Harvey, his rage grew—until it finally emerged full blown and he became a roving, prowling killer intent on gratifying his own murderous fantasies. He became a carefully programmed killing machine, but one who could mimic human responses cleverly. He was able to approach women and girls in a disarming way and fool them into thinking that he was safe. He was even able to make Eileen Hunley see him as a pious Christian whom she could love. Despite his weathered, furrowed face, Harvey could be charming, and like all antisocial personalities, he was oddly brilliant. His intelligence manifested itself in cunning and subterfuge, and all his energy was channeled into his obsession: revenge against women.

Harvey was not insane, not in the legal sense, and not in the clinical sense. He simply had no conscience at all. And that was a defect that could no longer be remedied.

Harvey faced a maximum sentence of thirty years in prison on the aggravated sodomy conviction, and a twenty year maximum on the attempted murder conviction.

However, Harvey's trials had only begun, and sentencing in the Gwen Burton trial was delayed until after he stood trial on the assault charges levied in the Jerri Billings case.

Declared competent to stand trial in that case, Harvey Carignan was back in court in Hennepin County in the first week of April, charged with four counts of sodomy and indecent liberties in the September, 1974 attack on thirteen-year-old Jerri Billings. This time the presiding Judge was District Court Judge Crane Winton.

As a witness, Jerri Billings was not a prosecutor's dream. It had been almost two years since she suffered her nightmarish ordeal in the cornfield, and she faltered on the specifics of times and places.

Jerri testified that she could no longer remember the exact day in the fall of 1973 when she had accepted a ride with a man in the pickup truck. When the defense asked why she had not reported the attack for some time, she replied that she was afraid.

"I was on the run; I thought I would be arrested if I went to the police."

In order to show a commonality of plan, a pattern of action, Assistant County Attorney John Brink sorely needed the testimony of other alleged victims of the big man with the hammer.

Judge Winton *did* allow the testimony of all the women who had survived to report the attacks perpetrated on them: Gwen Burton, Lisa King, June Lynch, Sally Versoi, Diane Flynn, and Marlys Townsend (the woman who had been saved because she wore a wig). They all paraded to the witness stand and recalled their encounters with Harvey.

According to the witnesses, Harvey Carignan had carried out his reign of terror in Minnesota from June 1973 until he was apprehended on September 24, 1974. They made an impressive showing.

Once again Harvey took the witness stand himself. He denied ever having seen Jerri Billings before.

"I have never been with that girl," he said firmly. His insanity appeared to be under control now. He did not mention God, nor God's messages to him to obliterate harlots and whores.

Rather, he was concise and rational when he said he had never owned a light-colored truck. "That truck was red when I bought it. At the time she says she met me, I'd painted it bright yellow and black."

On April 18 the jury found Harvey guilty on all counts against Jerri Billings.

Judge Winton voiced bitterness that this trial had ever taken place, insisting that Harvey already had so many years hanging over his head from the Burton trial that the Billings trial was an unnecessary burden for the taxpayers in Minnesota.

True, perhaps. In Minnesota, no one can be sentenced to more than forty years in prison, no matter how many convictions he piles up, no one except a felon convicted of first-degree murder, which carries a life sentence. Harvey had faced only technically a *fifty year* maximum going into the second trial.

The defense, not surprisingly, agreed with Judge Winton.

The prosecutor—Gary Flakne, Hennepin County Attorney, did not. "There were seven victims who wanted to testify against him, they were entitled to their day in court too."

More than that, Flakne wanted to make a point to state parole authorities. Citing the number of violent criminals who had been released too early, Flakne said, "One way to impress the parole board is to have a number of long sentences to demonstrate that this is not a one-shot deal, but a number of cases."

When it came to attacking young women, Harvey Carignan could hardly be considered a "one-shot deal."

On May 5, 1975, Harvey Carignan was sentenced to thirty years in prison by Carver County Judge Haering on the sodomy charges involving Gwen Burton. After his sentencing in Chaska, he was then driven immediately to Minneapolis where Judge Winton sentenced him to a second thirty year sentence for the sodomy inflicted on Jerri Billings. Sixty years on paper, no more than forty years in truth. No matter how many crimes he was convicted of, statute decreed that he would not serve more than forty years.

Adjudication in the hammer murders of Kathy Shultz and Eileen Hunley lay ahead.

18

Harvey had been on the front pages of Minnesota papers for nine months; suddenly new information surfaced that promised he would remain in the headlines throughout the summer of 1975.

One of the biggest crime stories in Minnesota had begun on July 27, 1972, when Virginia Piper, wife of Harry C. Piper, Jr., chairman of the board of the Minneapolis brokerage firm of Piper, Jaffray, & Hopwood, Inc., was kidnapped from her plush Orono, Minnesota, home. The brokerage firm headed by the kidnap victim's husband was the largest investment firm in the Midwest, and the Pipers were often seen on society pages, publicity that made them attractive targets for kidnappers and extortionists.

When Virginia Piper's husband came home to an empty house, a house where his wife was invariably waiting for him after his day's work, he had been frantic. After an agonizing wait, contact was made with Piper, and a ransom demand was made: "one million dollars—to be paid in fifty thousand unmarked twenty-dollar bills."

Mrs. Piper's family had had, of course, no way of knowing if she were alive or dead, but they arranged to have the million dollars in twenty-dollar bills dropped at the specified spot.

Two days after she was abducted, Virginia Piper was found, unharmed, chained to a tree in a wooded area near Duluth.

Although she had not seen her kidnappers' faces, she had

managed to peek beneath her blindfold and catch a glimpse of their feet. There had been two men, men who seemed tall and strong from the way they pushed and pulled her along.

During the time that Mrs. Piper was held captive in the Jay Cooke State Park in Duluth, she had complained of being cold, and one of the men had given her a sweatshirt to wear; the shirt had been emblazoned with a monogram from St. Olaf's College. She didn't think that her kidnappers were alumni of the Lutheran college, but she remembered the shirt. She also had managed to sneak a quick look at the car she was taken away in, and described it later as a two-tone model. A two-tone vehicle *had* been stolen from the customer-service lot of Larson Chevrolet on July 11—sixteen days before the kidnapping.

One of the men—the man who had been with her the most—had worn "Red Wing" shoes.

This information might mean little to the man on the street, but to cops it meant that they were probably looking for an ex-con. Red Wing shoes are prison-issue shoes, and every con sent away from the walls at Stillwater has worn Red Wings shoes.

"Anything else?" Mrs. Piper had been asked. "Anything else you saw or heard?"

"The man in the Red Wing shoes wore his pants rolled up at the bottom."

This bit of information, along with Mrs. Piper's recollection of conversations, would not mean much for three years.

The man who had stayed with the kidnapped matron while his cohort went to pick up the ransom money had talked a good deal with her. Just as she'd memorized his shoes and the way his work pants were rolled, she'd tried to memorize his voice so that she would recognize it if she ever heard it again.

He had talked about the hardships of children, about children who were abandoned by their parents, children who were abused and mistreated. He had also discussed the Northwest, and seemed particularly well-informed about Oregon and Washington.

This hardly narrowed it down for the detectives and the

FBI special agents who sought the kidnappers. There had been thousand of men issued prison shoes, a great number who wore their pants rolled up, and just as many who had a soft spot for abused children. Perhaps there were not as many who had traveled to the northwestern portion of the United States. . . .

When Archie Sonenstahl had come across the maps in the old pickup truck that had formerly belonged to Harvey Carignan, he had tried to break the code of the scarlet circles. He'd discussed them with Duane Homan and Billy Baughman, and the conclusion reached was that the circles could quite possibly represent a number of things. The circles around Whidbey Island and the Tulalip Indian Reservation surely marked where Harvey had killed Laura and Kathy. The other circles in Washington had netted no bodies, although the circle in Medora, North Dakota, had.

"Those circles in Minnesota," Homan had speculated, "might only be places he'd looked for work. He kept writing to Alice that he was driving all over looking for work in construction, and he wasn't doing that well. Maybe he just marked off the places where he'd already tried."

Well, now Sonenstahl knew that some of the circles matched where victims had been attacked, but there were still some that had not been explained.

Some of the Piper ransom money had been passed, a trickle of twenty-dollar bills appearing mainly in southern Minnesota and in Brooklyn Park, near Minneapolis.

On a hunch, Sonenstahl compared the circles with the spots where the ransom money had been passed. *The circles matched!*

So Mrs. Piper's kidnapper had talked about the Northwest, about child abuse, and he'd worn Red Wing shoes and rolled-up pants. That was fascinating because Harvey invariably wore his pants rolled up. What was even more interesting was the fact that the woods where Mrs. Piper had been chained to a tree to await rescue were directly across the street from a farm in Duluth where Harvey had lived as a child!

But Mrs. Piper had never seen the faces of her kidnappers, so she wouldn't be able to identify them from a lineup. The only way she could identify them was by ear.

Sonenstahl obtained a tape recording of Harvey's voice. In Minnesota it is legal to record surreptitiously, and Sonenstahl recorded a conversation between himself and Harvey in the latter's jail cell. Sonenstahl then asked six FBI agents to repeat the same phrases that Harvey had used. When they had done that, Sonenstahl had a voice lineup.

Sonenstahl asked Virginia Piper to listen to the seven voices, each mouthing the identical phrases.

The Hennepin County detective watched her face carefully, and saw her tense as she listened to one of the voices.

Mrs. Piper asked to hear the voices again, and then said that the third voice was familiar. "That's him—that one—that's one of the men who kidnapped me!"

The voice was Harvey Carignan's.

Joseph Friedberg acknowledged to the media that the FBI had questioned Harvey about the Piper kidnapping, but said that his client denied knowing anything about it.

The FBI would neither confirm nor deny that such questioning had taken place. However, Friedberg said that Harvey had told him the special agents had said they knew Harvey had paid his lawyers with Piper ransom money.

"We were not paid in Piper kidnap money," Friedberg said firmly.

Friedberg accused the FBI of "playing cop games" and hinted that they had promised Harvey amnesty for all of his rape and attempted-murder sentences if he would tell them where the Piper ransom money was.

The Minneapolis *Star* printed rumors that Harvey and a close relative were thought to be involved in the Piper kidnapping and said that Harvey had been fingered after an unidentified woman said a drawing of one of the kidnappers looked like a person closely associated with Harvey.

Although the headlines blossomed, Harvey was not indicted on charges connected with the Piper case. There might still have been time; the statute of limitations on kidnapping would still be in effect until 1977—*if* officials could come up with enough evidence proving that there was interstate transportation connected with the kidnapping.

The money itself—whatever was left of the million-dollar

ransom—would forever be "poison money." The penalty for knowingly passing ransom money is ten years in a federal penitentiary and a ten-thousand-dollar fine.

The "Piper Chapter" in Harvey's story would never become more than a mass of speculation. The money, beyond the small percentage passed in 1972 and 1974, never surfaced. Harvey would never acknowledge any connection with the crime. In the end, the case amounted to a bizarre probe in which many possible suspects were questioned and in which one witness was alleged to have told the FBI she could locate the ransom with a crystal ball.

Could Harvey have been involved? Possibly. The Red Wing shoes, the rolled-up pants legs, and the conversations about the Northwest and abused children sound like Carignan. The fact that the victim was found so close to Harvey's boyhood home seems odd. And yet the M.O. is different from his violent crimes; Virginia Piper was terrified, but she was not physically harmed.

It is a question that may never be answered.

19

While the kidnapping investigation disappeared into a morass of seemingly unprovable speculation, and while he had been sentenced to two thirty-year terms in prison (of which he was required to serve only forty years) after two trials, Harvey still had other charges hanging over his head. The sex murders of Eileen Hunley and Kathy Schultz waited unavenged.

On June 19, 1975, Harvey was indicted by an Isanti County grand jury on murder charges in the killing of Katherine J. Schultz. Isanti County Attorney John Dablow met with the press and said that the grand jury had met in Cambridge that morning, and he speculated that the trial would begin in October. The indictment alleged that Harvey had killed the eighteen-year-old student by striking her on the head with a "blunt instrument." He was charged under both sections of the Minnesota first-degree-murder statute. One section involves premeditation and the other stipulates that the murder in question must have taken place during the commission or attempted commission of rape or sodomy. Harvey's alleged crimes fit into both categories.

On September 4, Harvey was arraigned on a second set of first-degree-murder charges, the murder of his girlfriend, Eileen Hunley. Again, both criteria for first-degree murder had been met.

After this second murder charge, handed down by the Sherburne County grand jury, Harvey appeared before Sherburne County Judge Robert Bakke. He entered no plea, and Judge Bakke continued the case until Harvey could consult with an attorney. A pretrial hearing was scheduled for December 1 on this newest charge.

Claiming prejudice because of widespread pretrial publicity, defense attorneys were granted a change of venue to Anoka County.

It seemed that Harvey's marathon legal hurdles might never end. Would further trials end with more judges crying that those trials had been totally superfluous and a burden to the taxpayers?

And yet, viewed from the victims' side, did not Kathy Schultz and Eileen Hunley deserve *their* day in court too? Certainly they would be silent witnesses, unable to tell a jury what had happened to them. Moreover, a conviction now might mean that Harvey would draw a *life* sentence.

Kathy Schultz would never have a day in court. Harvey pulled a surprise by pleading guilty to her murder.

Why Harvey chose to confess to Kathy Schultz's murder—when he had resolutely refused to discuss with police authorities the murders of Eileen Hunley, Kathy Miller, and Laura Leslie Brock—is as inexplicable as his convoluted personality.

Through plea-bargaining, the charges were reduced to second-degree murder. Attorney John Dablow said that he had agreed to the reduced charges because Harvey was already serving the maximum forty-year sentence and because he still faced first-degree-murder charges in the death of Eileen Hunley. Beyond that, Dablow said that testifying again would place a "grim burden" on the living women whom Harvey had attacked.

On February 9, 1976, Harvey waived his constitutional rights and took the witness stand. He admitted that he had picked up Kathy Schultz on September 20, 1974, in south Minneapolis when he spotted her hitchhiking. He then drove her to the cornfield forty miles north of Minneapolis—near Cambridge—where he killed her.

Judge Bakke asked Harvey if the blunt instrument referred to in the autopsy report had, indeed, been a hammer.

"No, sir," Harvey replied. "It was similar to a mountain-climbing tool or a trenching tool."

"Your crimes are so gross that there is no point in commenting on them—" Judge Bakke said as he pronounced sentence.

Harvey glared, and interrupted the judge. "Don't comment on them, then!"

Judge Bakke continued in his sentencing. Harvey was sentenced to forty years. He now had a hundred years of prison time hanging over his head.

It still meant only forty years.

The consensus was that Harvey would also plead guilty to killing Eileen Hunley. He had nothing to lose, and he had much to gain. By pleading guilty to the second murder charge, he might avoid a life sentence. Surely the murder of a young woman who had sought only to lead him into a religious life would stamp him as a heartless monster. The prosecution would play on that. And all of Harvey's biblical quotes could not mitigate the horror of Eileen Hunley's violent death at the hands of a man who had purported to love her.

But Harvey had never been predictable; he chose to go to trial in the Eileen Hunley case. Perhaps even he could not admit to what he had done to Eileen.

Once again a Minnesota jury listened to testimony on Harvey's propensity toward violence. They heard that Harvey and Eileen had had a three-month relationship, a relationship that ended with a falling-out. Harvey had maintained his allegiance to The Way—but not to Eileen.

And Eileen too had ended up in a lonely field, her head smashed into fragments, her body violated with a tree limb in a final humiliation.

The fact that Harvey had attempted to collect Eileen's last wages—even as her brutalized body lay undiscovered in the brush fifty miles from her empty apartment—did not bode well with the jury.

He would have had to know that she had disappeared, even if he were not responsible. And yet, he had not reported her missing; he had shown no concern for her at all. He had only tried to divert her last modest paycheck to his own uses. It hardly seemed the act of a concerned lover, or even of an ex-lover.

Harvey did not convince the jury. On June 24, 1976, he was convicted of first-degree murder in the bludgeoning death of Eileen Hunley, and sentenced to life in prison.

Harvey now had sentences totaling 100 years plus life, *but* they would run *concurrently*, and he could seek parole after seventeen years. It was still highly unlikely he would serve more than forty years.

Three years and twenty-three days had passed since Kathy Miller's body had been found. If she had not been avenged for herself, other women's deaths had, tragically, avenged her.

Harvey had garnered his share of headlines. He was infamous, literally one of a kind—a man who had escaped the punishment of the law for his worst crimes for almost three decades.

There were serious rumors that Harvey's lifetime of crime had attracted no less an author than Truman Capote. It was said that it was only a matter of time before Capote would arrive in Minnesota to chronicle Harvey's life—just as he had immortalized Dick Hickock and Perry Smith in his classic *In Cold Blood* after they had obliterated the Clutter family in Garden City, Kansas.

Harvey hinted at Capote's interest confidently, and there seemed enough substance to his claims and the claims of others to believe that Capote would record Harvey's life. But, for some reason, that book never came about.

Harvey, however, had studied journalism himself. He was a most literate man. His letters to Alice—letters that became part of police records—demonstrated that. His syntax, sentence structure, and use of detail and example were excellent, superior to those of most college composition students. He decided that he would write his own book.

And so, locked in Stillwater, Harvey varied his routine. He still worked on his body, doing his calisthenics and chin-ups. But he also began to write. Or rather, it is alleged that he began to write the story of his life and of the injustices done to him. No one can ever be sure.

In early April 1977, there was a massive shakedown in Stillwater, and much contraband was confiscated. Earl Guy, editor of the *Prison Mirror*, told the Minneapolis *Tribune* that one of the casualties was his mailing list for the paper. Guy said he had foreseen such an eventuality and that he had secreted two other mailing lists in the prison. But after the shakedown, all lists were gone—one from his cell, one from the *Mirror* office, and one that had been kept beside the *Mirror*'s Addressograph machine.

The *Mirror*, founded in 1887, is the oldest continuously published prison newspaper in the United States. However, its future seemed compromised in 1977 when both a typewriter and a typesetting machine used in its publication also vanished after the shakedown. (Despite the setback, the *Mirror* survived.)

Moreover, Guy said he had had an eight-hundred-page book manuscript that had disappeared. "Two other prisoners lost manuscripts," Guy claimed. One of the two was Harvey Carignan. How much writing Harvey had actually accomplished, or the subject of his book, was not specified.

Harvey's last bid for freedom came in 1978. The Minnesota Supreme Court heard his appeal. Two of the ruling justices raised a valid question—a question that struck fear into the hearts of Harvey's victims and the families of deceased victims. The justices wondered whether perhaps juries should be told what might happen if they were to acquit a defendant by reason of mental illness. Defense attorneys in Minnesota are not allowed to discuss the effects of an acquittal based on mental illness. Critics say that this allows juries to speculate that a defendant will go free, although this is not always the case.

Under Minnesota court rules, a defendant is not automatically sent to a state hospital if he is acquitted on mental grounds—but the court proceedings for commitment are begun.

"Since the court cannot prevent the jury from speculating on the results of its verdict, it should at least ensure that such considerations are based on accurate information," Justice James Otis said.

Still, although Justice Otis and Justice Rosalie Wahl had raised the question about just how much a jury should know when an insanity plea is introduced, the majority of the court said juries should not be told what procedures will be followed if they bring back a verdict of innocent by reason of mental illness, and the entire court unanimously upheld Harvey's conviction on August 11.

The insanity plea would, of course, continue to be an area of dissension in trials in America. In 1980 Ted Bundy, accused of the murders of two sorority girls and a thirteen-year-old junior-high-school student in Florida (and a suspect in thirty other murders), was allegedly offered a chance to plead guilty by reason of mental defect. Had he accepted the plea bargain, he would have avoided the death penalty—which he subsequently received in all three cases. In 1982 John Hinckley chose the "insanity" route in his trial for the attempted murder of President Ronald Reagan. He *was* found to be insane at the time of his crime and committed to a mental hospital—a decision that outraged much of the nation.

The insanity defense will undoubtedly continue to raise serious questions in America's justice system. It is questionable whether the M'Naughton Rule will continue to be the guideline for future jury decisons. One psychiatrist in Texas has announced to the media that he has launched his own campaign to destroy the insanity plea. He has stated that he testifies in every case for the side of the prosecution. "I've convinced the juries each time that the defendant was *not* legally insane when he killed."

And yet there are killers who have murdered while in the grip of true psychosis. It is not an easy problem to solve.

20

Fifteen years have passed since Kathy Sue Miller waved good-bye to her mother as she walked away from the bus. Today Kathy would be thirty years old. Instead, she is long dead—as are Laura Leslie Brock, Kathy Schultz, Eileen Hunley and Laura Showalter. No one can ever know what good they might have accomplished had their lives continued.

The other young women who were viciously assaulted by Harvey Carignan have picked up the pieces of their lives—but the memory of the terror they endured will never really leave them. They trust far less than women who have never been so grievously violated.

Jerri Billings, the thirteen-year-old runaway, was adopted by a Hennepin County sheriff's detective and grew up to be a fine young woman. Gwen Burton no longer shows the outward effects of the brain damage she suffered during that rain of hammer blows, blows meant to kill her. But occasionally, when she is very tired, she still has difficulty in forming her thoughts and expressing them verbally; she has a residual aphasia when she is fatigued. Dorcas Callen, one of Harvey's first victims in Alaska—the woman who fought him and managed to scramble out of the ditch in Anchorage—is a middle-aged woman now, living in Seattle. She still cannot speak of that attack so long ago without trembling.

Just how many women encountered Harvey Carignan probably will never be known. The faded red circles on the crumpled map of America may indeed represent burial spots.

Or they may indicate something else. One thing is certain. The prisoner himself will not offer information.

In 1983, Larry Wood, in charge of Special Projects for the Cable News Network (CNN) set out to do a documentary on serial killers in America. Part of his gripping project was a long interview with Harvey Louis Carignan. Carignan had discussed his crimes in the past only when he was in the throes of the "insanity" he blamed for his aggression.

Carignan agreed to an interview, an interview that would, of necessity, take place within the confines of prison walls in Minnesota. "I like your boss," Harvey told Larry Wood. "I like Ted Turner's style—I'll do it."

The interview was held in the Maximum Security prison in the Minnesota correctional system, a brand-new, "escape-proof" facility in Oak Park Heights. When that highly sophisticated facility was ready for occupancy, Harvey had been one of the very first prisoners to be transferred from Stillwater. On February 16, 1983, he and a number of other hardcore, proven violent prisoners were moved to Oak Park Heights.

Wood had been told that Harvey Carignan was a big man, but even so, he was not quite prepared for the very tall, thickly-muscled prisoner who was issued in and seated at the far end of the shiny waxed conference table that separated the interviewer from the interviewee. Harvey wore a cream-colored cowboy shirt with a blue/black pattern and pearly studded buttons. He leaned back in his chair and seemed to peer down at Wood as if from a great height.

He did not smile. Harvey Carignan's voice was a deep boom, and he weighed each question posed to him with deliberate slowness before he responded.

The camera crew stood behind Larry Wood, but it was easy for him to forget they were there; it seemed that he and Carignan were alone in this carpeted room with its narrow bulletproof windows. Save for his subject, it might have been a boardroom for a corporation. A profusion of houseplants bloomed behind Harvey, and an ashtray, unused, sat in front of him.

Whenever Wood asked a question that Harvey Carignan

did not choose to answer, he leaned forward and stared directly at the reporter, his huge shoulders hunched so that he looked even larger. Invariably too, Harvey's left eye would begin to twitch when the questions moved too close to areas he wanted to avoid: his relationship with his mother when he was a child, any possible feelings of rejection that he might have, the lack of female companionship in his teenage years—and most definitely, the subject of Kathy Miller.

And yet surprisingly, this man who was clearly eminently sane, wanted to talk about aspects of his life heretofore hidden.

"If there wasn't that something about me that gets me into trouble—that kept me from getting ahead, I just have a feeling that I would have been a hell of person," Harvey began. "Whenever I am at where I can get ahead, I always get ahead—I'd generally wind up with the best there is, without hurting others; that's what it's supposed to be all about—"

Harvey admitted that he supposed the blame for what he had done was ". . . mine, in the long run. (But) a person grows up and becomes what he is due to the things that happen to him—and maybe he himself caused some of them and maybe other people caused others, and maybe his brain doesn't function just right. At times, I see apparitions; I have hallucinations, but they haven't bothered me for a long time. But when I see them, I'm a very dangerous person."

Locked up, he considered that he was just "a normal, everyday person that happens to be in jail. . . . I'm not dangerous now, but I won't say that I wouldn't be tomorrow."

He had thought a great deal about that "other person" who sometimes took over his body, and he had come to realize that some of the things he had done, he had really wanted to do—but the other person was the one who was in charge of his body at the time.

It is a theory much espoused by criminals when they are captured, and the concept of multiple personalities in one body is currently intriguing to forensic psychiatrists. The drawback is that so few criminals ask for help with the other personalities who are tormenting them until they are arrested.

Thereafter, multiple personality disorder is a popular, but rarely successful defense.

When Harvey Carignan picked up thirteen-year-old Jerri Billings and drove her to the isolated field, he told her that his name was "Paul." Now, as he recalled his very early childhood, he mentioned the name again.

"From the time I was a very young child—and this is very young . . . I'd say two or three years old—I had an imaginary friend. His name was Paul. He had the same clothes I had, the same toys I had. Everything I did when I was by myself, it seemed as if he was with me. He was always the person that would get me into trouble. One time the painters were painting the house, and he dared me to throw dirt against it, so I took the dare and I did it, and I was into trouble. It was things like that. I'd do things like run into fences and get cuts because I'd be playing with him. I'm sure my parents knew about it, because I can remember my mother telling me one time, 'You damn fool. You've got to quit pretending.' I was very young 'cause we moved out of that house before I was five."

"Paul" stayed with Harvey, he recalls, until he was eleven or twelve, and then he left when Harvey went to reform school. Later, Harvey remembered other voices, but never again "Paul's." Was it deliberate—or unconscious—when the grown-up Harvey told Jerri Billings that his name was Paul?

Harvey's eye twitched rapidly as he related another incident that he felt had contributed to the kind of person he had become. For the first time, he revealed that he had not spent all his teen years in reform school. He said he had gone to live with a farm family, but that arrangement had ended precipitously with his return to reform school.

Harvey Carignan described the farmer as "a degenerate—" a man who engaged in bestiality with his farm animals, and neglected his wife. The wife in turn, Harvey recalled, had seduced him—this fourteen-year-old hired boy. The farmer, enraged, had taken Harvey back to the reformatory, and claimed that Harvey had raped his teen-age daughter.

From that point on, Harvey Carignan had remained in the

reform school until he was of age. There were occasional dances, where town girls edged timidly in to dance with the bad boys. "I never got to really feel what a girl was like," Harvey remembers. "Oh, their arms and their hands, but no more than that. . . ."

Harvey Carignan, going into his 36th year of institutional life, on videotape, is a fascinating image. He is obviously bright, and yet he shows the lack of cause-and-affect reasoning so often found in a sociopath. His demeanor is humble and compliant on the surface, but just beneath, there is an angry, wary man. One moment he guesses that he "probably" would be dangerous if he was back on the streets. And moments later, he muses that he will one day be free.

He speaks calmly about the crimes for which he has been convicted—with the exception of the abduction of Jerri Billings, which he vehemently denies. Why? That is the abduction where he was "Paul."

Harvey had never really explained the death of Eileen Hunley, the shy, religious woman who had fallen in love with him. Now, even as he serves his sentence for her murder, he relates a most bizarre version of her last moments.

He was having hallucinations, he felt, at the time Eileen disappeared. He had been "down to Ohio and got mixed up with some weird religious kooks in a cult, and somehow or the other, they got it through my mind that no matter what a person had done or what he wanted to do, he was already forgiven for it—and stuff like that.

"I was looking for Eileen for a couple days—she had disappeared. And one day I went up to her house and the house was open, after it had been locked for a few days. The position of the blinds had changed so I knew someone had been coming there. I heard someone calling me . . . and it dawned on me that it was her. I looked around and the only thing I could see was a white van, so I went over to it. I asked the guy sitting in it, 'Do you have someone here by the name of Eileen?' and he says, 'No, why don't you get yourself the hell out of here before you get yourself in trouble.' He tried to hit me through the window, so I pulled him out and knocked him down, and I walked around to the back of the van, and opened up the door and there she was. I remember as clear as anything she had on a pair of knee-length pants and a wet t-shirt—that's all she had on—and she said, 'Harvey, these guys raped me.' ''

But Harvey hadn't really believed Eileen. Her clothes were too neatly folded over her arm, and she held her shoes in her hand.

Even so, he helped her out of the van, he said. At that point, one of the men inside drove away, and the other had crawled over and had bitten Harvey on the leg. ''I shook him and knocked loose some teeth when I kicked him.''

And then he couldn't believe it, but Eileen had jumped on Harvey's back, yelling, ''Leave him alone!''

''I just went berserk. I remember reaching around and grabbing her hair, and pulling her over my shoulder. And the next thing I knew—I mean the next thing I could *control*—I was helping her into my car, sitting her on her clothes. I was gonna take her to a hospital. But, she just stiffened out—and she emptied her bowels and her bladder and I knew she was dead—so I just stopped right where I was and put her in the trunk, and cleaned out my car and threw her clothes out. . . .''

Harvey's voice is laconic as he justifies the killing of Eileen Hunley, and berates the trial where this information ''never came out.'' His very lack of feeling is telling. But he doesn't realize what he had revealed. His face is calm, his huge hands relaxed on the waxed table top.

And then, suddenly, his words became rapid, his voice alive, as he talked about murder, ''I don't care what a person does or how he does it—there's a certain excitement. The excitement might not be a thrill, but there's the excitement. I was very excited because she had jumped on my back to help the other person I was saving her from. . . . She had jumped on me to save the person who had supposedly raped her and I was angry.''

But not now. No anger here as Harvey Carignan stares down the table into the cameras. He is explaining. The sociopath believes that he can explain *anything* if he only talks long enough and persuasively enough.

The only question posed to Harvey that elicits immediate rage, quickly subdued, is one about Kathy Miller.

"There is no Kathy Miller," he says flatly, and he leans forward heavily, glaring into the camera and at his interviewer, Larry Wood.

Harvey will not, *will not*, talk about the murder of Kathy Miller. He has been voluble in discussing Eileen's death, and quite frank about other attacks against women. But he turns inward when asked about Kathy. Finally, Harvey admits that he did talk to someone on the phone, someone who said her name was Kathy Miller and asked for a job. "I told her to come down and I'd give her a job. She said it was too far away and she didn't knew where my gas station was at."

Harvey recalls that he told her he would be in her neighborhood the next day, and that he told Kathy he would meet her, but that he never got around to getting there. He had never seen her.

Harvey Carignan admitted quite calmly that he deserved to be in prison, but objected to testimony and published accounts of his crimes which accused him of sodomy, battery, and forcing women into his car. It was his contention that his victims had gotten into his car without a fuss. It seemed to be a point of pride with him.

"Do you think that it would be the best thing for you to be locked up for the rest of your life?" Wood asked flatly.

"It wouldn't be the best thing for me—but it might be for other people. . . ."

And so at last, Harvey Carignan: McNeil Island #22072-, Alcatraz #935-AZ, Leavenworth #78025-L, Washington Correctional Center 125096, Stillwater #k-9419, and F.B.I. #335 123 A, Seattle Police Department #79642, King County Sheriff's Department 68559, Spokane Police Department #01071, and Renton Washington Police Department #13679, seems to have found a permanent prison home.

Perhaps.

Harvey Carignan is eligible for his first parole hearing on May 8, 1993. He will be sixty-six years old in 1993. Of those years, he will have spent forty-five of them behind bars.

*   *   *

Mary Miller still lives in the same house she once shared with Kathy and Kenny and her elderly parents. They are all gone now but Kenny. Kenny has tried very hard to understand why his sister went away, and all subsequent losses of relatives and friends hit him doubly hard. Mary still works at the bank, and she continues to devote her free time to the Families and Friends of Missing Persons and Violent Crime Victims. She has traveled to a dozen states to advise new chapters, and testified before the United States Senate Judiciary Sub-Committee on victims' rights, as well as appeared on national television specials.

Kenny Miller works in a sheltered workshop. He is nearing thirty, and he no longer makes up stories that his sister got married and lives in California. He has learned what the word "murdered" means, and has forced himself to say it out loud. He is very tall and handsome, and is still given to bringing home what his mother calls "strays—people and animals who have nowhere to go."

All three of the detectives most instrumental in bringing Harvey Carignan to trial have retired. But each of them worked for years after the Carignan investigations, despite a period of illnesses that can be traced directly to the stress of the months of frustration. Duane Homan had a bad back, Bill Baughman developed ulcers, and Archie Sonenstahl suffered a coronary. These are the classic medical problems that hit homicide detectives; the human mechanism can cope only so long with the tragedies of others before something has to give.

Recovered, Homan, Baughman, and Sonenstahl worked hundreds of homicides after Harvey Carignan was finally safe behind bars. Bill Baughman retired from the Seattle Police Department in the early 1980s and now works on the security staff at the Washington State Legislature. Duane Homan retired from the Seattle Police Department in late 1987.

While I was researching this book, Duane Homan and Bill Baughman talked about Harvey Carignan for the first time in years.

Carignan had insisted that the two Seattle detectives had

fired a shotgun at him, deliberately trying to kill him. It never happened. But there were moments when they wished they were back in the days of the Old West in Washington Territory, and not hampered by the precise rules of law and modern civilization.

"It's a terrible thing to say," Duane Homan mused, "But I almost wish that Harvey had pulled that hammer on us when we went out to tow his car away that day in 1973. No officer ever wants to shoot someone—but . . . if we'd had to kill him then, think of the young women who would have lived. If it had ended that day, none of the Minnesota crimes would ever have happened."

Baughman nodded. "I had my gun out of the holster. I was that close to shooting. It looked like he was going for Duane, and I couldn't have let that happen. And then his hands came out empty, and the moment was over."

And so it was. And so Harvey Carignan continued in his consuming vengeance against females.

"One thing," Homan said, "one thing I've wanted to do for years—and I'm going to do it now."

Duane Homan retrieved the stack of dusty files on the Kathy Miller case from the vault at the Seattle Police Department. He opened one of the brown accordion files and turned to the last page. In a firm hand he wrote, "January 31, 1983—This case is closed: 'Exceptional.' The killer of Katherine Sue Miller is presently incarcerated in the Minnesota State Prison."

And then the files were tied up again and taken back to the vault. Legally, the last notation would change nothing, but the three lines would show that the Seattle Police Department had marked Harvey Carignan down as Kathy's murderer.

Harvey himself has scarcely deteriorated in prison. It is his milieu. He knows prison far better than he ever knew the world outside. His rage clearly still lives within him, but outwardly, he has changed little. He is still a physical fitness fanatic, and has put on weight. The man whose rap sheet reads, "capable of superhuman strength" still is.

Other cons admire him for his intellect, and he served as

editor of the Stillwater Prison newspaper before he was transferred to Oak Park Heights.

Harvey Carignan's life is full of coincidences, a bizarre kind of synchronicity. The officer he confessed to in Alaska at the time of his first murder was named "Herring," and the judge who sat in the trial where he was convicted of murder in Minnesota some 27 years later was named "Haering." Harvey murdered two young women named Kathy. He murdered two women named Laura. It is unlikely that he deliberately chose his victims by name. His mother's name was Mary, and neither of his wives were named Kathy or Laura. His victims were chosen at random—because they were women, vulnerable, and easy to abduct—and yet there are the unexplainable commonalities of names.

In prison they call him "Harv-the-Hammer." Few of the convicts are brave enough to say it to his face, but you can hear it whispered along the prison hallways and in the mess hall.

And an odd thing has happened. The lines and scars of Harvey Carignan's forehead have combined in such a way that he carries with him always the mark of his crimes. Between his eyes, there is now a perfectly balanced "H."

"H" for "Harv-the-Hammer."